HOW TO SAVE THE WORLD
IN YOUR SPARE TIME

HOW TO SAVE THE WORLD IN YOUR SPARE TIME

ELIZABETH MAY

KEY PORTER BOOKS

Library and Archives Canada Cataloguing in Publication

May, Elizabeth
How to save the world in your spare time / Elizabeth May.

Includes index.
ISBN-13: 978-1-55263-7814
ISBN-10: 1-55263-781-6

1. Social action—Canada. 2. Environmental protection—Canada—Citizen participation. 3. May, Elizabeth I. Title.
HN107.M39 2006   361.2'0971   C2005-906813-2

The publisher gratefully acknowledges the support of the Canada Council for the Arts and the Ontario Arts Council for its publishing program. We acknowledge the support of the Government of Ontario through the Ontario Media Development Corporation's Ontario Book Initiative.

We acknowledge the financial support of the Government of Canada through the Book Publishing Industry Development Program (BPIDP) for our publishing activities.

This book is printed on acid-free paper that is Ancient Forest Friendly (100% post-consumer recycled paper).

Key Porter Books Limited
Six Adelaide Street East, Tenth Floor
Toronto, Ontario
Canada M5C 1H6

www.keyporter.com

Text design: Martin Gould
Electronic formatting: Jean Lightfoot Peters

Printed and bound in Canada

07 08 09 10 5 4 3 2

*In memory of my mother, Stephanie Middleton May (1928–2003),
who taught me everything I know about saving the world.*

"The hand that rocks the cradle rules the world."

ACKNOWLEDGEMENTS

This book is the result of years of experience and dozens of Sierra Club of Canada activist-training workshops across Canada. I have enjoyed each and every one of them and learned a great deal from the hundreds of participants. I thank all those who have taken part as well as the whole team of fabulous campaigners at Sierra Club of Canada—Stephen Hazell, John Bennett, Bruno Marcocchio, Rachel Plotkin, Dianne Pachal, Angela Rickman, Katie Albright, Daniel Green, Ken Madsen, Emilie Moorhouse, Lisa Matthaus, Colin Campbell, Lindsay Telfer, Emily McMillan, Selene Cole, Dan McDermott, Jamie Kirkpatrick, and Jason Bull. Our fabulous volunteers are too numerous to mention and thank, but I am particularly indebted to the national board for all their support.

My work on this book has benefited from Sierra Club of Canada's researcher, Cendrine Huemer, and Executive Assistant, Debra Eindiguer. The *Bush Briefing Book* was brought to reality through the creativity of Richard and Jo MacArthur at Junior Design, based on my writing and vague direction for what it should look like. Thanks to Ken Rubin. Special thanks to Glen Davis for copy-editing as well as helping us chalk up another "miracle" victory in December 2005 in averting a drilling decision for the Arctic National Wildlife Refuge.

Thanks to Anna Porter, who accepted this idea when she was heading up Key Porter, to Jordan Fenn, and to my editor, Jonathan Schmidt, who has been such a delightful (and light) editor.

Lastly, and always, I thank my daughter, Victoria Cate May Burton for her unimaginably generous love and support.

Contents

Introduction

AT TEN THOUSAND FEET, THE FORESTS of New Brunswick looked like the Robert Louis Stevenson poem about the little boy sick in bed, surveying his kingdom, "The Land of Counterpane." A patchwork quilt, over knobby knees and toes, a range of greenish hues with ribbons of blue, spread out below us.

I was in a small private plane, well-appointed as a tubular living room, travelling with Jim Irving, CEO of J.D. Irving Ltd. Irving has christened itself "the tree-growing company" in New Brunswick, operating logging on 4.2 million acres to feed the voracious appetite of its own Irving pulp and paper industry. As we flew over the landscape, Jim Irving pointed out the family holdings and Crown leases; pretty much all we could see was in Irving control. I observed to him that few people could fly over the land and be the master of all they surveyed. The thought seemed to mildly surprise him.

We spent the day in the remote north western holdings of J.D. Irving Ltd., touring the Black Brook forest area. Sierra Club of Canada had challenged the granting of certification to Irving's Black Brook holdings by Forest Stewardship Council (FSC). We argued that Irving's logging was not of sufficiently high ecological standards to merit this market benefit. It was a difficult day, agreeing to disagree on some matters, appreciating progress where progress had clearly been achieved. All in all, I decided Jim Irving was a hell of a nice guy who may actually have enjoyed the company of someone who was not sycophantically agreeing with him.

We headed back toward the airstrip crammed in an eight-seater van, with Irving staff and consultants in the rear, me in the front passenger seat, and Jim Irving at the wheel. He asked if I had come to New

Brunswick solely for our meeting. I confessed that I had already had another full-day workshop organized in Moncton for the next day.

"What kind of workshop is it?" he boomed. (He pretty much always seemed to be on full volume and high wattage.)

"It is an activist training workshop," I answered, wondering how he would absorb the concept, "You know: 'How to Organize,' 'How to Lobby,' 'How to Get Media Coverage'...I call it Democracy 101."

"Democracy 101?" he roared, "Well, I've never really needed that!" and then, as his press assistant reddened, he laughed long and loud.

It is a fact of life that corporate CEOs do not fret about getting a meeting with the Minister of Whatever. If you are perceived as powerful, access is assumed.

In a democracy, however, all citizens should be powerful. Unfortunately, that power is more theoretical than real, unless and until citizens get organized. Making democracy work requires effective citizenship. It is not enough to vote every few years. It is not even enough to send a cheque now and then to an environmental or anti-poverty group.

Making democracy work *is* work.

Chapter 1
DEMOCRACY 101

IN RESPONSE TO MANY REQUESTS FROM small volunteer groups across Canada, over ten years ago I started holding activist training workshops for Sierra Club of Canada. I have held workshops in church halls, community centres, and hotel rooms from coast to coast to coast. I have tried to help stay-at-home moms frustrated that they cannot get city hall to create safe play areas; teachers who cannot stand new provincial curriculum rules and want to know how to change them; fishermen trying to get the federal bureaucrats at Fisheries and Oceans to recognize that the level of catch they have approved is too high to ensure a sustainable fishery. On the surface, these folks have little in common. They do have one essential common denominator: they are citizens in a democracy.

People want the tools to protect a favourite forest from logging or to keep a hospital or school from closing. The tools of democracy are equally effective for many causes and movements. I've seen "sos" work as a slogan for "Save Our Seas" as well as "Stop Overseas Sales" (of nuclear reactors) and "Save Our Schools." Issues whether large or small, municipal or international, all require a dedicated group of strategic and committed activists in order to succeed and shift a pending decision.

There is really no mystery to "fighting city hall." Left, right, or centre, organizing for change is about putting a case together, getting the word out, persuading the public that your cause has merit and finding ways to translate that public support into pressure on governments.

Unfortunately, these are not skills taught in school. Increasingly, even the basic civics 101 of how legislation is passed and the fundamentals of how government works, are omitted from core education. Too few people can easily name their municipal councilor, congressmen in the U.S. or member of the provincial and federal Parliaments in Canada.

Fewer people vote in elections. More assume that one person cannot really do much.

THE REALITY

The reality is far different. One person can change the world. We know the names of the heroes—Martin Luther King, Mahatma Gandhi, Ken Saro-Wiwa, Rachel Carson, Chico Mendez, Nelson Mandela, Dianne Fossey. To be a hero in that company requires a moral courage few of us possess. An alarming number of them were martyred for their beliefs. But there were others. Rosa Parks did not sit down in the "whites only" section of a bus in Alabama in a random act of exhaustion. She had been trained as an activist at the Highlander Center in North Carolina. She and many, many others had learned the principles of non-violent civil disobedience.

There is a catalyst. There is a spark. And then there are the thousands of unsung heroes who make change happen.

Would apartheid have ended, would Nelson Mandela have been freed from his jail cell on Robson Island to be the president of a free South Africa, if not for the mundane organizing of countless thousands of supporters globally? Churches, human rights groups, average, everyday folks hounded corporations to divest themselves of investments in brutal, racist South Africa. Would apartheid have ended if thousands of Canadians had not cared enough, if Prime Minister Brian Mulroney, a fellow Tory and ideological twin to Maggie Thatcher, had not thwarted her to lead the charge for a Commonwealth denunciation of the government of P.W. Botha? Would Nelson Mandela have ever been free if not for the letter of the one hundred thousandth person to the right target at the right time?

Who changed the world: Nelson Mandela, or you?

MY MOTHER STOPPED GLOBAL NUCLEAR WEAPONS TESTING

Maybe you thought it was President John F. Kennedy who stopped the testing of nuclear weapons in the atmosphere. Reality is, it was my mother.

In the late 1950s the famous "Ban the Bomb" movement started. The now ubiquitous peace sign was not mere graphic art, but a clear representation, using the nautical symbols, to indicate the letters: N. D. The peace sign is actually a semaphore sending the message "Nuclear Disarmament."

Mushroom clouds were routine when I was a toddler. We didn't see them in Connecticut where I grew up. They were in Los Alamos, New Mexico—a long, long way away. We had to test nuclear bombs in the atmosphere because it was the Cold War. You were better "dead than red." If the cost was a bit of radiation...well, only a commie would complain about that. But still the strontium 90 from the nuclear blasts, ionizing radiation with a mind-numbingly long half-life, fell back down to those amber waves of grain. The cows ate the strontium 90 in the grass. The cows' milk had radioactive nuclides. So the U.S. government's Atomic Energy Commission dutifully tested the milk from cows on the way to market. They reported the radioactive materials on the side of the milk carton as "Sunshine Units." The sun, after all, radiates energy. It's good for you. How much better then to have your own little suns radiating from within?

I was a baby when my mom read something (goodness knows where) that said that some scientists were worried that nuclear testing and the atmospheric radioactive fallout would result in an increase in childhood leukemia. In those days, childhood leukemia was quite rare.

My mother started worrying. At first, she didn't think about trying to stop nuclear weapons testing. At first she wanted advice about how to protect her baby from the radiation. She started calling scientists at the university. One told her not to buy fresh milk. Buy powdered milk instead, as it has had more time for the radiation to dissipate. One told her that he wasn't really sure it worked, but he was grinding up calcium tablets and adding them to anything he could get his kids to eat: ice cream, powdered milk, cakes. Since strontium 90 mimics calcium in the human body, it gets routed to bones and teeth, where leukemia can start in the bone marrow. His theory was that by maxing out the absorptive calcium capacity of his children's bones, there would be no room for the poisonous calcium look-alikes. I still remember the chalky taste of ice cream loaded with real calcium to ward off the radioactive fallout.

One day my mom decided that grinding calcium tablets was not enough. She kept grinding them up, but she decided to do more. She and my dad formed the Connecticut Committee for a Sane Nuclear Policy. My dad had just started as a young accountant at Aetna Life and Casualty in Hartford. He was the committee's treasurer and secretary. My mom was chair. There were no other members.

The committee started with a petition campaign. The petition put forward the elements of the issue, key facts, well-cited by unassailable authority. It appealed to a moral objection to poisoning the land and killing innocents without the permission of any one, least of all the innocents.

How can two people, a young couple in a new town, generate thousands of names on petitions? My mom started by opening the Yellow Pages of the Hartford phone book. She let her fingers do the walking to the Clergy section. From Abruza to Zezo, she phoned ministers, priests, and rabbis. All day long she worked the old rotary phone. She repeated her prepared statement over and over again, until she thought she must be speaking gibberish.

"Hello, (Minister Cunningham, Rabbi Kessler, Father O'Hara), I am a volunteer working with the Connecticut Committee for a Sane Nuclear Policy, and I wonder if you would be willing to circulate our petition in your [church, synagogue]?"

Two years old, I worked with my play phone, "I want to speak to ministers, priests and rabbis. I have a 'tition."

She was a member of the Junior League. She was a lovely hostess at cocktail parties. She volunteered for local charities. She started every letter to the editor, "As a housewife, a mother, and a Christian…" She didn't just write to local papers. When she wrote a letter, she sent it everywhere: the *Los Angeles Times*, the *Charleston News and Courier*, the *Cleveland Plain Dealer*, the Houston and Dallas dailies. Pretty soon we started getting mail. Hate mail especially came from Texas. And then we started getting crank calls late at night, "Your house is surrounded. Come out with your hands up." My mom started taking the phone off the hook after 10 PM.

Other people called to volunteer. Petitions filled up. The Connecticut Committee for a Sane Nuclear Policy had volunteers, and meetings with a larger executive. One day my mom thought, "It must be illegal to kill people without their permission. It must be murder."

She decided that the brilliant editor of the *Saturday Review of Literature*, Norman Cousins, with his incisive editorials for world peace, might be interested in her theory. She phoned the magazine in New York and was amazed to be granted an audience.

She met with the surprisingly young Cousins. He heard her out and suggested he knew of a few other people who had a similar notion. Perhaps he could let them know of her interest?

Once back home, a few weeks later, she received a letter from a lawyer representing an international law suit against the governments of the United States, the Soviet Union, and the United Kingdom. It asked if she would be willing to join seventeen other plaintiffs. By now, my mother had developed a much cherished, if local, reputation. She wrote that she would need to know something about the other seventeen plaintiffs as she had to protect her credibility and that of the Connecticut Committee for a Sane Nuclear Policy. A very polite letter came by return post listing the other plaintiffs. They were all Nobel laureates. The lawyer closed, "By the way, none of the other plaintiffs have inquired about you."

And so it came to pass that my mother entered a new phase—mass media. Her fifteen minutes of fame[1] came with the tag line "seventeen Nobel Prize winners and a Connecticut housewife."

I moved from playing with the toy phone to media prop status. Sitting on my mother's lap at the Washington, D.C., press launch of the suit to end nuclear weapons testing, I represented all the poisoned innocents of the world. At nursery school, I warned the other children not to eat the snow because it contained strontium 90. They didn't listen. They had only been warned not to eat yellow snow. I marched and picketed the White House, secretly hoping that Caroline Kennedy would come out to play.

By the time President Kennedy signed the Treaty Banning Nuclear Weapons Tests in the Atmosphere, my mother had built a movement in Connecticut, which joined a national organization. There were, in fact, hundreds, if not thousands of other worried American mothers.[2] The new national organization was called the Committee for a Sane Nuclear Policy, and later, just SANE.

My mother sat on the SANE board with Norman Cousins, Dr. Benjamin Spock, Norman Thomas, Homer Jack, and others. My little brother and I grew up knowing these leaders. Cousins became "Uncle Norman" and Thomas—multiple candidate for president and likely the only socialist to hold his own in U.S. politics—was dubbed by my little brother, "Normous Thomas." Geoffrey, at four years old, was sure that that must be the man's name, for enormous he was. (Geoffrey used to do an imitation of "Normous Thomas" in the bath—a sight which he had once beheld in awe—featuring knees to the chin, a frugal use of water, and a methodical use of soap.)

Before I turned eight, nuclear weapons testing in the atmosphere had been banned. I had watched as my mother spoke to one hundred thousand people from the plinth of Nelson's Column in Trafalgar Square at the closing rally of the Aldermaston March; as she went on a six-day hunger strike in front of the Soviet Mission to the U.N. in Manhattan to protest Soviet bomb tests; and came to know the famous, great and infamous. She loved Connecticut's liberal Republican senator, Prescott Bush (George W.'s grandfather from a much deeper end of the gene pool), had been the subject of Vice-President Nixon's flirtatious charm (she used to swear that he was very charming if you like that "what's a pretty girl like you worrying your head about nuclear weapons? Let me take you lovely ladies out for a drink" sort of line), and came to be friends of the likes of Bertrand Russell, Linus Pauling, and Hubert Humphrey (who held me on his lap through much of that press conference), as well as hundreds of other average, everyday folks who banded together with the goal of changing the world.

And they did.

LESSONS LEARNED AT MY MOTHER'S KNEE:

1. My grandmother always said, "Thought without constructive action is demoralizing."
2. You can accomplish anything you want if you don't care who gets the credit.
3. There is no one so famous or important that you cannot pick up the phone and talk to them. Even famous people need baths.
4. Media coverage is fickle.
5. Sometimes governments lie.
6. No one is powerless without their own permission.
7. Be polite.
8. Thank people for helping.
9. Changing the world is only a matter of time (if you have enough people on your side. Getting them on your side is what takes time!).
10. My mommy changed the world. So can I.

Chapter 2
GETTING ORGANIZED

LET'S FACE IT: WE ARE BUSY. Each of us has a million things to do, and the last thing on our minds is forming a citizen action group. Then, something happens to turn that comfortable, if hectic, world upside down. It may be a threat of some kind: a mega-hog farm next door, a big-box store crowding out a traditional neighbourhood, an incinerator threatening to spew out toxic chemicals, a new highway expansion, or clear-cut logging in the watershed. It could be a government-announced tax cut that will reduce home care for seniors. Or a utility that changes its policies about shutting off essential services for poor families. You are outraged. The thought runs through your mind: "Someone ought to *do* something!"

It may not occur to you immediately that that *someone* is you!

My first essential piece of advice is to skip the initial stage of hand-wringing frustration. Do not waste time lamenting that there is nothing you can do. Get busy! Find out who else in your circle of friends or larger community is also outraged. Meet for a coffee. Send out an e-mail to all the other Sunday school teachers on the roster at your church or to all the other dads who take turns driving the boys to hockey tournaments. You are likely not alone.

Maybe you do not want to work in a team and would rather run a solo campaign of letters to the editor and meetings with your local councillor. With the advent of electronic communication, it is now possible to launch a major mobilization from your laptop. Cleverly designed Web pages *can* impact public opinion. Mass e-mails calling for action can be the catalyst for actions around the world. Nevertheless even short-term efforts, such as Move On (www.moveon.org) end up becoming long-term groups with staff and funding issues. Most often, even lone wolves end up in packs when you take on a campaign that needs winning.

Working on your own will make sense if you want to stir the pot (complaining about erosion of the universal health care system), or rely on the work of others who are lobbying for health care reform. Working on your own in a viral campaign can work to keep people in cyberspace aware of your issues, but will not, without other efforts, work to shift public opinion or reach policy makers. Even people who appear to be acting on their own have at least some support. Craig Kielburger, who at twelve, took on the Canadian Minister of Foreign Affairs over children in sweatshops; or Terry Fox in his valiant run across Canada to raise money for cancer research, were not entirely alone. If nothing else, their lone campaigns were supported by family and friends. Eventually both spawned large and permanent efforts promoting their ideals. No activist is an island.

Maybe someone has already organized a small core group. Working in a group will make sense if you are working on an issue with a specific decision-maker (mayor and council, governor, provincial cabinet), there is no other group to rely upon and the threat is imminent.

Suddenly, there are evening meetings at homes of people you hardly knew before. Everyone is talking about how to get media attention, organize protests, and wondering about getting a lawyer.

You have to get organized.

Over the years, a number of books have been published to provide guidance to citizens who want to protect a special place—or, indeed, the whole planet. The first one I ever bought was *Ecotactics: The Sierra Club Handbook for Environmental Activists.*[3] In 1970 I was in high school and the handbook had just come out. I picked up my old well-worn paperback copy the other day. The introduction is great: "ecotactics (e-ko tak tiks) *n. pl.* the science of arranging and maneuvering all available forces in action against the enemies of the Earth. There is this to be said about *ecotactics*: you won't find it in any dictionary—not yet. Give it time."

Well, it's been thirty-five years or so, and ecotactics are still not taught in school. It is hard to know where to turn for answers to the most basic questions that face neophyte citizen's groups: Do you need to incorporate? Elect an executive? Raise funds?

It is hard to know where to turn for help. Local volunteer efforts tend to feel isolated. It is easy to imagine that no one had ever gone through the ordeal you are now facing. Truth is, millions of people have been there before. Take a deep breath and follow these steps.

Look around and see if an existing organization will help you. Can you appropriate an existing group to your immediate need? Many groups with some staff and capacity would be happy to help a group of volunteers prepared to do a lot of the work themselves.[4] Seeking some likely allies is a good first step.

If you decide to form your own organization from scratch, be careful not to allow the process of group creation to drain your energies. If your campaign is likely to be waged over a few months, or even years, you may not need to become incorporated at all. Arguing over by-laws is a sure-fire way to stunt the growth and enthusiasm of any group.

Organize to meet the needs of the group, not some abstract notion of what an organization "should" look like. There are no "shoulds." In the grassroots movement that over a four-year campaign prevented aerial insecticide spraying of Cape Breton Island, we never incorporated, we never elected a chair or an executive, never wrote a budget, and never opened a bank account.

I have found over the years that citizen's groups often leap to the assumption that they should incorporate. The provincial Societies Acts are researched and forms are filled out, without stopping to ponder, "Why are we doing this? Is becoming a corporate body really important to our campaign?"

It is a question worth answering. The philosophy of a corporation and the structure designed to facilitate it is antithetical to grassroots activism.

SHOULD YOUR GROUP INCORPORATE?

A history lesson on corporations may seem an odd place to start your tutorial in changing the world. Nevertheless, the structure of your group is a fundamental issue that has bedeviled many a neophyte organizer. Corporate structure was designed to suit business needs and accountability to shareholders. The legal fiction of a corporate "person" was invented to allow directors to protect their personal assets from corporate financial meltdown. How else would wealthy merchants take a chance on a corporate risk? Corporate structure was designed to allow explorers and adventurers to attract capital. Christopher Columbus might have sailed off the end of the flat Earth. No one knew. To encourage risky investments, the corporate "person" was invented by the king, and now protected by the state. None of that really fits the picture of a local citizens' group taking on city hall.

There is also an unfortunate dynamic to electing an executive. Those not elected may feel less responsible for the effort. More work will fall to a few. The "titles" can get in the way. Occasionally, someone actually begins to feel like, or worse, *act* like, the "president" when their role is really one of equal among equals.

Still, every group needs someone to take notes of decisions (the minutes of the meeting), someone to guide and steer the conversation (the chair), and someone to keep track of the money (the treasurer). Other than the treasurer role, those functions can be rotated from meeting to meeting. Sharing the taking of minutes is fair. Having a different person each meeting to chair the discussion can work well (if someone is dreadful at it, at least you have not elected them as permanent chair!) If someone is particularly good at it, the group can decide to keep that person in the role of facilitator. I have known of meetings where someone is appointed to be a "mood monitor" to flag accelerating tensions and defuse them, or to suggest a stretch break for nodding heads.

In other words, you need not decide to follow formal group organizational patterns. Pick the approach that works for your group at the moment.

Sometimes, an organization must follow corporate rules and clear those hurdles. Long-term accountability, certain funding sources, will require it. Other times, an organic, "form follows function" approach will work just as well and conserve energies for the fundamental goal.

Pete Seeger, folk singer extraordinaire, once gave a wonderful workshop on grassroots organizing at a conference we held in Ottawa. He had mounted a brilliant campaign to clean up the Hudson River. Starting in 1969, Seeger sailed his 106-foot sloop, the *Clearwater*, all the way down the Hudson, stopping in towns and cities from upstate New York to the island of Manhattan, preaching the gospel of saving the river. It worked. In every town in which he held a concert, an organizing committee was left behind. Each committee concentrated on the pollution around its little section of the river. Each little committee was fortified in the knowledge that it was not alone, that day by day and week by week the movement to clean up the Hudson River was growing.

Seeger's advice to organizers was "never have the kinds of meetings that only attract the kind of people who like going to meetings." He suggested meetings should be planned around a social event: a potluck supper, then a meeting, and after an efficient exchange of information and approval of the next campaign step, anyone with musical instruments should bring them out and everyone should sing. (This organizing approach is perfect if Seeger is your organizer.) Still, those with lesser gifts can appreciate sharing music, singing, dancing, and finding ways to build community between and among those folks with whom you are suddenly spending a lot of time.

My addition to Seeger's advice is "don't hold meetings if you have no reason to hold a meeting." If there is no need for a group decision, if the meeting is just to review financial statements, wait until there is a good reason to pull people together. Don't wear your team down with unnecessary meetings. If you follow that practice, your volunteers will know it is important to come to every meeting. They will know there wouldn't be a meeting unless there was an important decision to be taken.

THE POTLUCK SUPPER

A quick word on the potluck supper. Dr. Ursula Franklin, one of Canada's leading thinkers, professor emeritus at the University of Toronto, peace activist and Quaker, has extolled the potluck supper as the women's way of organizing. No one has to do all the work. Everyone contributes something. It is always delicious and whoever hosted the event gets great leftovers. Another wonderful organizing trick of the potluck supper is that everyone who is expected feels *obliged* to come. You might want to back out as the fatigue of the day catches up with you, but you promised that salad! If someone is only committed by saying, "I'll try to get there," anything could come up to keep them away. Even asking someone to bring the cream for the coffee becomes a bond far harder to break than a casual acquiescence.

MEETINGS SHOULD BE FUN

Already your skin is crawling. Meetings are never fun. The goal of "fun meetings" is an oxymoron. But think about it: how are you going to take on the challenge of stopping that mega hog barn, shopping mall or whatever? Your only resource is volunteer energy. You cannot afford to drain and deplete that energy every time you get together.

Napoleon said, "An army marches on its stomach." (We've covered that with the potluck supper.) Gertrude Stein said, "If I can't dance, I don't want to be in your revolution." Dancing is good for the soul.

If meetings are deadly, it is hard to keep going. Think about the physical space in which you meet. An airless basement room, even if "free" from the local community association, is not free. People need light and air to think clearly. Sitting in a circle is more conducive to creativity than sitting in rows. Move meetings around to different homes. Use church halls (big kitchens and lots of space for a supper or dance).

If you are in it for the long haul, make sure you create a space before or after the work is done to share and laugh. It is okay to digress slightly for a funny story. It is more than okay; it helps effective organizing. A forced march through a pre-set agenda does not inspire enthusiasm. The most important thing you can accomplish in a meeting is to re-charge the emotional batteries of the people you need to accomplish miracles before the next meeting.

Remember, effective organizing is about *building relationships*—the relationships between members of your group, relationships between your group and the media, relationships with people who may become donors, relationships with the people who make decisions. The central theme of this book is that you need to remember that you are cultivating relationships.

I have often wished that of the ten million or so species on this planet, we had the option of organizing among a less difficult one than *Homo sapiens*. Organizing whales might be great. Human beings all suffer from the same problem: human nature. I have never known of an organization, be it a big downtown law firm, a parish council, or an environmental group that did not suffer from the same affliction. So, be prepared. Know that interpersonal conflict, jealousies, silly cliques will form. Recognize that dealing with these problems is not extraneous to the task ahead. It is essential. Do not ignore the personal. Remember the 1970s feminist slogan, the "personal is political." Well, the political is also personal. Don't step on toes. Remember the magic words "please" and "thank you." (Just because this is a revolution, no one said you could be rude. As a feminist, I also think I can be a lady.) Try to diffuse potential squabbles before they erupt and waste peoples' time.

One of my favourite stories of diffusing potential personal strife occurred in the 1950s at one of the small nuclear disarmament groups in England. Feeling that the group was losing its focus, the chair asked each member of the group in turn to stand and share why they were personally motivated to end nuclear weapons testing. The room was, as usual in such efforts, a bit of a mismatch. There were young people, academics, mostly left wing; and a few older, more traditional, social conservatives. As they made their way around the room, the group of people who months before would not have had any reason to gather, or even speak to each other, shared their most heartfelt motivations for wanting a better and safer world. It came time for a very distinguished older woman, pearls and hat in place, to stand. She held herself with great dignity and said, "I want to see an end to nuclear weapons testing so that I will never have to see any of you dreadful people again." Her comment was met with wild applause.

MAKING DECISIONS

It used to be accepted that all meetings of organizations ran by *Robert's Rules of Order*. No decision was a decision until a motion had been made and seconded, amendable by friendly amendment with permission of mover and seconder, subjected to a *majority vote* and on to the next item.

Clever use of these rules can be nearly a guerrilla tactic, as in this excerpt from Des Kennedy's humourous recounting of a fictitious forest campaign.[5] Here's the set-up:

A small gardening club has become the lightning rod for controversy after adopting a resolution supporting preservation of Kumquat Sound. At its next regular meeting, a crowd of pro-logging rowdies with a new interest in the gardening club show up, and Caitlin, the group chair, opens the meeting:

I should like to call this meeting of the Upshot Island Garden Club and Horticultural Society to order. We'll begin, as always, with a reading of last month's minutes. Elvira.

Elvira stands up and reads the minutes in a voice that seems to tremble on the brink of a deep precipice. She gets to last month's motion about the club sending a delegation to Kumquat. Just at that moment a fierce male voice bellows out, "Bullshit!"

Silence stuns the room. Elvira stumbles to a halt. Heads turn in the crowd and a confused murmuring breaks out. It's Hunter Dreeb who's yelled.

Caitlin smiles directly at Hunter. "We'll accept additions or corrections to the minutes after Elvira's finished reading them," she says, ever so sweetly.

Hunter says, "Bullshit!" a second time, much quieter though, almost to himself, and subsides against the wall, apparently prepared to await another provocation before erupting further....

"Now," Caitlin says, one hurdle cleanly leapt, "business arising from the minutes?"

Geoffrey Munz rises with great solemnity from his chair, as though the College of Cardinals had just elected him Pope. He's wearing his country squire tweeds.

"Madame Chair," Geoffrey begins, clearing his throat, "concerning the Kumquat issue. I should like to move a motion."

"Please do," Caitlin smiles, as though she's been awaiting no greater pleasure all day long.

"I move," Geoffrey intones solemnly, like Winston Churchill over the BBC, "that the Upshot Island Garden Club and Horticultural Society deplores and renounces the illegal actions of certain of its members at Kumquat Sound, and that it rescinds and holds null and void its earlier motion authorizing any member to commit illegal acts as official representatives of this organization."

Geoffrey sits down to a round of vigorous applause, foot stamping, whistling, and shouts of "Right on!"

"Thank you," Caitlin smiles at Geoffrey. "Do you have the motion, Elvira?"

"I'm not sure I've got it just right," Elvira says. "Was that 'deplores and renounces' or 'deplores and denounces'?"

"I believe, Madame Chair," says Geoffrey, rising again on a point of clarification, but looking rather absurdly like Count Dracula rising from his coffin, "that the motion reads 'deplores and denounces.'"

Peewee, sitting right beside me, instantly shoots his hand into the air. "Yes, Peewee?" Caitlin says.

"Madame Chair," Peewee always talks fast at meetings, "I believe the mover said quite distinctly 'deplores and renounces' when the motion was moved. And this makes far more sense than to say, as he now does, 'deplores and denounces,' because deploring and denouncing are somewhat redundant, whereas deploring and renouncing indicates both a judgment about the activity in question and an actual withdrawal of support for it, which, unless I'm mistaken, is the intent of the motion."

"Thank you, Peewee," Caitlin says. "Does the mover of the motion agree that it read 'deplores and renounces,' or would you like to stick with 'deplores and denounces'?"

You can hear scattered groans across the crowd.

"Madame Chair," Geoffrey's back up again, twitching in his tweeds, "I believe the intent of my motion is perfectly clear. Frankly, I'd like to both denounce and renounce this whole sordid affair." A smattering of clapping accompanies this sally, though plainly the complexities of the case are already beginning to muddy the previous clarity of certain people's convictions.

"Am I to understand," Caitlin asks, still smiling beatifically, "that you want to amend the motion to include both renounce and denounce?"

Geoffrey"s momentarily nonplussed, and Peewee leaps to his feet in the breach.

"Point of order, Madame Chair," Peewee calls.

"Yes, Peewee?"

"Madame Chair, the motion has been duly moved but not yet seconded, and I don't believe the rules of order allow us to discuss amending the motion until it is seconded." Peewee sits down with a wonderful gravitas, as though he's just been awarded the Nobel Prize in physics.

"Quite right. Thank you," Caitlin says. "Is there a seconder for the motion?"

Several arms shoot into the air. Elsie Pitfield's recognized as seconder.

"Now," Caitlin says, "it has been moved and seconded . . ."

"Point of order, Madame Chair!" This time it's Fibber Miller on his feet. Fibber has never been known to set spade to soil, but his many land transactions have given him a certain expertise in legal matters.

"Yes, Mr. Miller?" Caitlin seems to be enjoying herself in this procedural quagmire.

"How can the motion be seconded," Fibber asks, "when we haven't yet determined what the wording of the motion is?"

Caitlin runs us all around the track a few more laps, entertaining motions to amend, to withdraw, to table the motion, ruling that only the mover of a motion could move that it be tabled, that no new motion could be moved, seconded, or discussed while an existing motion is on the floor. Elvira gets herself into a complete muddle as to what's being moved by whom. Elsie Pitfield keeps calling "Question!" trying to force the vote forward, but at every turn a new procedural hook snags us, as though we're trying to beat our way through a copse of thorny brambles. Arms are shooting up and down as everyone scrambles to grab a bit of turf through points of order and procedural refinements. In the entire hubbub, we never quite get around to addressing the gist of Geoffrey's original motion, which is by now amended beyond recognition.

The sweet irony in all of this is that it was Geoffrey himself who had, while he was president of the club, introduced the cumbersome rules of order that are now throttling his motion.

Sierra Club of Canada board meetings still follow that basic structure to get through a long agenda, but changes have been introduced. Most decisions are reached by consensus decision-making. The issue is discussed and at a certain point an agreement begins to congeal. At that point an effective chair tests for consensus. Confusion can defeat this method of decision-making if the decision is not stated and then subjected to the test. Consensus decision-making need not be fuzzy. A group can arrive at clear decisions by either method.

The advantage of consensus decisions is that the whole group will feel some ownership of the direction set. On really important issues it is very important to ensure that the whole group understands and agrees. If, for example, the issue is whether or not to hold a demonstration in front of the legislature, the success of that effort requires that the entire group is supportive. If the *Roberts Rules of Order* method is used and the vote to hold a demonstration passes by a narrow margin, those who thought it was a bad idea may just not participate. Worse, they may decide to leave the group. Those who favoured the motion may not be able to deliver a successful demonstration without every single member of the group calling every single one of their friends to get the word out. It will be cold comfort to those who won the vote if the event falls flat due to a lack of group solidarity.

As a key organizer, you should go into a meeting with a clear plan of what you hope to accomplish. It is essential that you have energy and excitement around a particular proposal and have done enough advance homework to keep the discussion from bogging down. If you are suggesting having a table in a mall to collect names on petitions, you don't want people wondering if a table is allowed in a particular mall to allow collection of petitions. Momentum is created if you can say, "I phoned and made a tentative booking for a table at the farmer's market next Saturday. It costs twenty dollars and there is no charge if we cancel. I just wanted to be sure we could have the table if the group decided it was a good idea." If you have all the details thought through and have answers for all likely questions, energy is much more likely to be directed to the right target: accomplishing the goal; not arguing about its merits.

While consensus decision-making works most easily in groups of fewer than twenty people, with a basis of mutual trust from previous experience, it can be used in groups of several hundred. This was famously the case at the 1993 Clayoquot Peace Camp. The valiant local group, Friends of Clayoquot Sound, based in Tofino, British Columbia, had been formed to protect a spectacular coastal area of Vancouver Island—a series of pristine islands, cloaked in old-growth temperate rain forest. Industrial clear-cutting in Clayoquot Sound was destroying watershed after watershed. Taking the thousand-year-old trees from steep slopes was causing landslides. Despite years of effort in mobilizing to save Clayoquot Sound, in the spring of 1993 the British Columbia government decided to allow logging to continue throughout most of the sound.

Desperate measures were required. The Friends of Clayoquot Sound put out a call for people willing to join logging blockades. Valerie Langer, one of the key organizers, remembers that they had had no idea if anyone would come. By the end of the summer nearly one thousand people had been arrested in non-violent civil disobedience, staying on the road after an injunction was read to leave or face arrest. Many thousands more came to the area to help. Langer and company set up a peace camp, based on the model of the women's peace protest at Greenham Common in the U.K. They set up rules for peaceful coexistence. They fed and housed thousands of people in a clear-cut. They had music: Australian rock band Midnight Oil, and children's performer and eco-troubadour Raffi. They maintained an impressive level of self-discipline. The code of non-violence prohibited even responding to the taunts of the industry provocateurs brought in daily to verbally abuse the protesters.

Eventually, through the 1993 blockades, market actions in Europe (persuading major paper purchasers in Europe to reject B.C.-sourced products until Clayoquot Sound was protected), and a series of innovative negotiations with the industry (under new management) and First Nations, most of the pristine areas of Clayoquot Sound will never be logged.

Of the many extraordinary aspects of what was dubbed the 1993 Clayoquot Summer protests was that decision making continued to be by consensus, even as the numbers grew. The group developed a system of hand signals to send messages to the group silently. (Several hundred people really cannot talk at once if you are trying to come to a decision). The "twinkling" method (fingers high in little rippling motions) allowed the organizers to gauge the level of support for various ideas. The discussions could go on into the night, leaving them sleep deprived as they formed the morning's blockade in the pre-dawn cold and chill. Still, I have never heard anyone engaged in the Clayoquot Summer protests suggest that they would have done better with majority vote, or a small steering committee announcing decisions to the larger whole.

TIPS TO ACHIEVE CONSENSUS:

- Try to review issues openly.
- Let the discussion make its way around the issue.
- Let it double-back and find a new perspective.
- Let everyone offer their opinions.
- Never force a result.
- Trust in letting a good decision rise to the surface. When it does, watch to see the opinions congeal around it. As people begin to repeat the same points, being "in violent agreement" as one of my friends puts it, bring the discussion to a close and test for consensus.

Don't react negatively to a new idea. Who knows? Even if you have done your homework for a particular strategy, another idea might be better. Or you could do both!

If someone makes a suggestion that you feel sure would be a waste of time, do not say so. Do nothing to disempower your team. You want everyone to stay energized and active. So, if there is a proposal that sounds lame to you, as long as it couldn't be a detriment to the group, say, "Good idea! Can you take that on?" (Quite often, some people in a group will be critical of what others are doing or not doing, and suggest a great number of ideas that they have no intention of delivering themselves. Call their bluff. Let them take on that project. Who knows? Maybe they will deliver. If not, you have lost nothing.)

CREATIVITY AND INSPIRATION ARE MORE IMPORTANT TO CAMPAIGNING THAN BUSINESS PLANS.

How can that be? Business plans and budgets are essential, but a truly brilliant idea will make all the difference in the world. It is not a waste of time to arrive at decisions with which everyone agrees. This process can take longer than conventional majority rule. Keep your sense of humour!

THINK ABOUT WHAT PEOPLE NEED

Organizers of groups need to listen to the needs of the members (and prospective members). If someone explains that they can never come to a meeting on Wednesday nights, remember that and avoid scheduling conflicts. If anyone in the group has small children, think about babysitting help. In our early Cape Breton organizing against aerial pesticide spraying of the forests, the meetings were always at my house. It was an accident of fate (or not) that my family lived in a house next to the main highway with a large easement at the beginning of our driveway. It guaranteed that in winter months when driveways could be hidden behind a mountain of snow, ours was accessible. We had another big advantage over some of the other key organizers. We had running water and electricity. So our meetings also featured the bathing of children and the doing of laundry. I have no idea how much that helped attendance at meetings, but it didn't hurt. Planning to meet peoples' needs also meant that the logistics for a major anti-spray conference in Halifax required

lining up people who would stay behind. A key function of the conference included the people who tended other people's wood stoves and fed their animals so more rural residents could make the trek to Halifax.

For most modern-day organizing, livestock issues may not come up. But, childcare is a universal and often ignored aspect of meeting planning. If meetings advertise the availability of childcare, more people will be able to participate. The price of a babysitter for the evening is well worth it if it encourages people who care to be able to attend. (Better yet, find out if anyone in the group has a teenager who will look after little ones as their donation to the cause.) Keep the meeting place wheelchair accessible. Figure out if there are people who can offer rides to others who might otherwise not attend due to transportation problems. Make sure you have been inclusive in your planning. Keep everyone involved.

The late Senator Robert F. Kennedy had a cardinal rule for political organizing: Never tell a volunteer you have nothing for them to do. If need be, invent something. Have a list of things at hand that a new volunteer can do for the group. Do not give an untested volunteer the task of organizing your next press conference. Delegate sensibly. For a volunteer's first assignment, pick a task on which nothing critical depends: clipping items from the newspapers; delivering petitions to more locations than you really need; things that are a "plus" without being a "must."

In thinking about what people need, you should ask yourself, "Why is this particular person here?" For some the answer is obvious. (They get their drinking water from the watershed that is about to be clear-cut. They are downwind from the proposed incinerator.) For other issues, for instance the anti-globalization movement, the threat is just as real, but more indirect. Some people may have come to your group seeking a social support network (they want some friends). Some may come because they want to be a hero (please send me to the barricades). Some come because they are service oriented (they really do only want to help). Figuring out what your volunteers really want and helping them find it is an important way to build your organization. Not everyone wants to be publicly thanked. They become unhappy and embarrassed. Others cannot live without it. Pay attention to what motivates your team. Find ways to keep them motivated.

CESAR CHAVEZ

One of the great grassroots movements of all time was the 1960s effort to secure the rights of California farm workers. Migrant workers, mostly from Mexico, were brought to California seasonally to pick the fruit for North American supermarkets. It would be hard to imagine people less powerful in the system than migrant farm workers. They were being paid a pittance, worked long hours, lived in appalling conditions, and were often directly exposed to overhead pesticide spraying. The workers formed a union, the United Farm Workers (UFW). But unlike the industrial model where a strike of organized labour could cripple the employer, the migrant workers had no bargaining power. If they went on strike, they would be easily replaced. The major fruit companies were impervious to their demands. The movement's prime organizer, Cesar Chavez, knew that his only hope for decent working conditions lay in reaching the consumers, the customers of the big employers.

The challenge was monumental. The union had no money. It had no power. Many of the members could not even speak English, much less run a stunning media campaign. But somehow it started. The "Boycott Grapes: Support the UFW" movement spread. I remember it as a defining aspect of my childhood. In Connecticut, we stopped eating grapes in support of the farm workers in California. I remember seeing friendly supporters of the farm workers conducting information pickets outside grocery stores. I remember the bumper stickers. Against all odds, through the mid-1960s to early 1970s, the campaign and the movement took hold, until finally the big fruit companies had to back down and accept the workers' demands.

Chavez was once asked, "What is the secret to success in organizing?" He answered, "The only way I know how to organize people is to talk to one person, then talk to another person, then talk to another person."[6]

LESSONS LEARNED:

1. First step in organizing: plan the victory party!
2. Be creative.
3. Be persistent.
4. Keep your sense of humour.
5. Support each other

6. Watch your energy level. Avoid doing things more than once that drained energy.
7. Don't be forced into someone else's mould.
8. Sometimes follow *Robert's Rules of Order*. The rest of the time, stick to Roberta's Rules of Disorder.
9. Keep everyone involved.
10. If you are the key organizer, you need to be one part leader, one part psychiatrist, one part visionary, and for the rest a very hard worker!

Chapter 3

CHOOSING YOUR GOAL
(OR, HOW WILL YOU KNOW WHEN YOU'VE WON?)

THE KEY TO EFFECTIVE CAMPAIGNING is for the collectivity of people working on the issue to share exactly the same goal. They may share the goal out of different motives or through a different process of reasoning. Nevertheless, the core goal, the outlines of victory, must be clearly shared.

One may assume that everyone in a committee to protect a particular ecosystem through park creation, or a group committed to eradicating pesticide use in a neighbourhood, has exactly the same goals. But what if a park is proposed by the government that would protect only 75 percent of the ecosystem, or a proposal comes forward to eliminate herbicides, but not insecticides. Are you all *ad idem* (in agreement)? Does everyone agree that the goal has not been met?

You need to be able to clearly enunciate what you want. This helps identify the decision-maker (local, provincial, state, or federal government, or corporation) that can deliver your victory (your key target). You should be able to close your eyes and *see* your victory. As a matter of fact, creative visualization of exactly what you want helps your focus. (Creative visualization may also be able to change events. No one knows for sure, but it works for me. Prayer never hurts.)

Be sure to choose your ultimate (long-term) goal, and some shorter-term ones as well. Achieving a few short-term goals early in a campaign (such as the number of people you attract to the cause, the number of names on petitions) builds momentum and confidence for the longer-term goal.

IS IT WINNABLE?
A number of handbooks for activists suggest an initial survey of the opposition's resources versus your resources. This pragmatic approach

urges the citizens' group to review its position and demonstrate that the campaign is winnable. Tally up your resources and then look at the other side's strengths.

Imagine Cesar Chavez facing such a calculus: "Let's see. They have all the money: they control our lives, they can vote, the politicians are all their friends. For our strengths: we have no money, no power, we cannot vote, and we don't know anyone but other migrant labourers." Or the French Resistance versus the Nazi occupation. Or the small band of rural Cape Bretoners taking on the oldest incorporated firm in the world and government-approved plans to spray insecticides from airplanes. When examined rationally, none of these efforts had a chance. Yet, all of them were victorious.

"Is it winnable?" may be the world's most pointless question. Our assets are not quantifiable. Persistence, passion, and commitment will outrun mere money every time.

The biggest and most despair-laden question is the *big one*: "Are all our efforts too little, too late? Is the planet so damaged by human-caused pollution—toxic wastes, ozone depleters, greenhouse gases—that no matter what we do we are doomed?"

Get a grip! This is a dangerous frame of mind. It provokes nothing but grief and drains your energy into sheer paralysis. Philosopher George Grant once told me, "The greatest sin is the sin of despair."

Playwright John Gray spoke at a Vancouver environmental conference a number of years ago and ranted about whiny environmentalists who bemoan our fate and ask whether it is already too late. "No one can know. Do you think our parents' generation knew that Hitler was slated to lose? Did they sit around and worry that there was no point in confronting fascism because it was already too late? .... We don't know if we are winning or losing and it is pointless to ask."

We have to do what we have to do. Miracles happen. The life force of this planet is very strong. Dandelions poke through sidewalks. We don't know enough to give up. We only know enough to know we have to try to change the course of human events.

THE ART OF THE IMPOSSIBLE

Politics has been described as "the art of the possible." It is all about compromise and balancing interests. Never make the mistake of thinking the role of the citizen activist is the same. Our role is the art of the *impossible*. Nine times out of ten, we will (and have) accomplished the impossible. Of course, if you do not try to challenge the status quo, the result is assured. Once an environmental group compromises, the chance of a complete victory is lost. The politician practising the "art of the possible" will never do more than environmental pressure groups are demanding. A compromise is a willing defeat.

You should never even *ask* if a campaign is winnable, because the question is not answerable. No one can predict the course of the future. Time and time again, I have seen completely unforeseeable shifts in the tide of events that result in a campaign victory (you could think of them as miracles or a Shakespearean plot devise: *deus ex machina*). Mark Twain was right when he said, "Truth is stranger than fiction, because fiction is obliged to stick to the possibilities." My aunt Mary was right when she said, "Life has much more imagination than you or I."

Although I could fill the rest of this book with examples of impossible goals being achieved, I'll contain myself to a couple of examples.

A SHORT COURSE IN MIRACLES

I remember one memorable meeting in a kitchen in Cape Breton in January 1997. I had driven twenty hours through winter storms from Ottawa to join this meeting. A group of local people were trying to plan a response to a recent government decision. The cabinet of Nova Scotia and Premier John Savage had decided to reverse proposed protected area status for Jim Campbell's Barrens in the highlands of Cape Breton, an area once part of the national park, in order to open it for mining.

Someone from Halifax (with lots of political insider knowledge of the Nova Scotia government) suggested that the campaign goal should be to ensure legislated protection for the other twenty-one proposed protected areas. He confidently explained, with a rational, logical, and entirely factual assessment of the views of the provincial cabinet, that there was no way to reverse the decision to allow Jim Campbell's Barrens to be mined.

True, none of the rest of us could offer a plausible scenario by which the area of bog and barren at the source of the Margaree and Cheticamp Rivers would be re-protected. But we were equally certain that we had to try. The odds were certainly against us. We didn't even have the advantage of an evocative name for our wilderness jewel. It always helps to be calling for the protection of something magical. "The Great Bear Rainforest, home of the Spirit Bear" is about right. "Jim Campbell's Barrens" fell far short of the mark.

We were up against a powerful array of political insiders who stood to benefit from the potential gold mine, including former Prime Minister Mulroney's close associate Fred Doucet. Despite the odds, the Committee to Save Jim Campbell's Barrens set its sights on the right goal: returning the area to protected status. We organized as a coalition, with national groups (Sierra Club of Canada and the Canadian Parks and Wilderness Society), local groups (the Margaree Salmon Association), and individuals. We campaigned and raised public awareness of the precedent-setting decision to turn a park into a mine.

Over the next eighteen months, a number of unpredictable events occurred. It was revealed that there had been an unprecedented level of trading in Regal Goldfields, the gold mining company with an interest in the barrens, in the hours between when the Cabinet decided to open the area to mining and when the decision was made the public. (Mark Twain was also right when he defined a "gold mine" as a "pile of dirt with a liar sitting on top of it.")

The RCMP and the Securities Commission launched an investigation. The premier decided to resign (in what was an unrelated personal decision), and a provincial Liberal leadership race resulted in a new premier taking control. One of the first things Premier Russell MacLellan did was to reverse the decision to open the Jim Campbell's Barrens and restore the area to protected area status. A great book relating the full story, still unpublished, was written by local filmmaker and key campaigner, Neal Livingston. He called it *Robber Barrens*.

Even more imposing odds faced the effort to protect the Queen Charlotte Islands from clear-cut logging. The vision of a South Moresby wilderness proposal was the brainchild of two young men—an American draft dodger kayaking around the islands and a young Haida artist. It was a summer party that led the two to be sleeping on a porch—or at least trying to sleep. They had not met before, but both were sleepless, worried about escalating logging in the islands' most awe-inspiring, ancient temperate rainforests. They got up and began strategizing. Deciding that they needed to leave some areas to the north for logging but protect the southern third of the Queen Charlotte Islands archipelago, they mapped a proposed protected area—from the height of land of the Tangil Peninsula, south to the tips of the southern most islands of the archipelago called Haida Gwaii.

In the middle of a summer night in 1973, they drew a line on a map and created a fourteen-year campaign to protect South Moresby.

The odds against them? Formidable. The logging companies had a very cozy relationship with the provincial government. Through the years of the campaign, the premier of British Columbia was usually of the far right. The Social Credit (Socred) governments of Bill Bennett and then Bill VanderZalm were hardly friendly to environmental goals. Western Forest Products wanted to log the last old giants. Industry's potential profits were in the tens of millions. A two-thousand-year-old tree is a lot of fibre.

Assets of the campaign's founders? They had a map and a pen.

By July 1987, the cause of saving South Morseby had been championed by every major conservation group in Canada, and by the royal families of the U.K and the Netherlands. Canada's leading environmentalist, Dr. David Suzuki and his popular CBC TV program *The Nature of Things*, took up the campaign. Haida elders had been arrested on the logging roads at Lyell Island, to the horror and shame of many Canadians. The House of Commons had passed an all-party resolution in support of saving the area. The then federal Minister of the Environment Tom McMillan, in a Progressive Conservative government, worked in close alliance with the NDP member of Parliament for the area, Jim Fulton, and a number of key Liberals, including former Environment Minister Charles Caccia. The Speaker of the House, John Fraser, referred to it as the "conspiracy to save the planet."

Ultimately, Prime Minister Mulroney personally negotiated saving the area directly with Premier VanderZalm.[7] As the negotiations reached their end game, the logging contractor sent his men into triple shifts, clear-cutting around the clock to log as much as possible. The logging reached the crest of a watershed called Windy Bay on Lyell Island, which conservationists had identified as the jewel in the emerald chain of islands. The chain saws were heard in Windy Bay where a Haida encampment waited for fresh conflict and blockades. But the blockades were never needed. Agreement was reached and logging was stopped.

What saved South Moresby was a core of dedicated people who knew, no matter what the odds against them, that they would succeed. It took never, ever, conceding. Even when it was reported on the national news that there would be no national park in South Moresby, that the British Columbia government would create a much smaller provincial park instead, the Save South Moresby team, now including the federal Minister of the Environment, did not give up. It took fourteen years and consumed the lives of John Broadhead, Thom Henley, Guujaaw, Vicky Husband, Miles Richardson, Colleen McCrory, and countless others. The young man who drew the line is now president of the Council of the Haida Nation. The area he drew is now Gwaii Haanas National Park. You should go there. It is the most amazing place.

One last example of stopping the unstoppable takes us to the Amazon. It took me there, quite literally.

In 1988, Paiakan, a young indigenous leader of a tribe called the Kaiapo, decided to stop a huge dam. The dam on the Xingu River, a tributary to the Amazon, was to be built downstream from Kaiapo lands, delivering power to a non-indigenous industrial expansion in the northern Amazon. It was an announced project of the Brazilian government. It had the support of the World Bank. It would flood hundreds of square kilometres of rainforest and threaten the Kaiapo way of life. Paiakan lived on the Xingu River in the village of Aucre, only reachable by small private plane or by days on a boat. His access to outside resources was limited to the one anthropologist who had taught him Portuguese.

One day a film crew from Canada came to his village working on a documentary on the loss of the Amazon. The film crew was from *The Nature of Things*. Paiakan met David Suzuki and told him of his vision for a protest against the dam. He wanted to bring together peoples from as many Amazonian tribal groups as possible in a pan-Amazonian tribal council against the dam. This had never even been attempted. The logistics alone were daunting. The tribes did not share a common language. They lived in the remotest places on Earth. And he wanted the demonstration to take place in the town that stood to benefit most from the dam, Altamira. It would be a hostile environment for a gathering of indigenous people.

The Amazon was on fire. The cbc-chartered plane couldn't take off because the smoke was too thick. When he finally reached a city and found a phone, Suzuki called his wife, Tara. Tired and grief stricken, he cried on the phone. Tara (one of my favourite people in the world) called me, panicked. Her husband had never cried on the phone before, so Tara was crying and she told me we had to raise a lot of money to help Paiakan with his demonstration. I didn't think twice about it. Neither did Tara. We started calling more people. We pulled together fundraising concerts in Vancouver, Toronto, and Ottawa. Gordon Lightfoot agreed to sing at the events. Everyone asked agreed to provide everything for free. Paiakan was invited to the U.S. thanks to the anthropologist who found a way to bring him to a conference in Miami. He agreed to add Canada to his itinerary. He added Europe. He had never worn laced shoes. He had never flown in a commercial jet, couldn't figure out how to open the bathroom door, and couldn't read the signs. He waited on a transatlantic flight to find a bathroom at the airport in Germany.

The concerts were accompanied by a letter-writing campaign. We asked people around the world to write the World Bank and demand that they not fund the Altamira Dam on the Xingu. After Paiakan's trip through Canada, I was told the department of finance had received more letters about stopping the dam than about de-indexing old age pensions.

We raised seventy thousand dollars for Paiakan's campaign, gave it to Paiakan, and then decided (Tara's idea again) to go to Altamira for Paiakan's demonstration in February 1989. Tara thought it would be wise to have some North American observers. We were worried about Paiakan's safety. Rubber-tapper activist Chico Mendes, working to protect the forest and organize a rubber tappers' union, had just been assassinated in the neighbouring province of Rondonia.

As we approached there were wild rumours in the Brazilian media that Brigitte Bardot would be coming, and even Sting. The group of us, a contingent of about thirty Canadians, including David and Tara Suzuki, Gordon Lightfoot, activist Paul Watson (of Sea Shepherd fame), a number of First Nations chiefs and leaders; and a motley crew of Canadian activists, found this hysterical. We were "in the know." Other than Lightfoot, we couldn't imagine any other celebrities would be in Altamira.

We had flown through Miami to Manaus, and from Manaus to Belem at the mouth of the Amazon. At the Belem airport we found all our seats had been given away or, more accurately, re-sold. Tickets to Altamira appeared to be going to the highest bidder as the Woodstock-like atmosphere of a possible Sting appearance gathered momentum. We split into smaller groups. The Belem airport began to have the mood of Vietnam in the fall of Saigon. We'd get on anything. Some of us made it onto flights through wait lists. The rest chartered two small private planes (they barely seemed air-worthy) for the flight to Altamira.

We arrived to the baking and dusty heat of the remote Amazonian town. Paiakan had succeeded. Tribal peoples from all over the Amazon had made it to Altamira by plane, bus, and boat. The indigenous gathering was in an enormous amphitheater. Tribes gathered together, in their varied feathered headdresses, their body painting, small monkeys occasionally peering from their owners' shoulders, children at their mothers' breast. It was like walking into a *National Geographic* article. It was a kaleidoscope of colour. At the front of the room a representative of the Brazilian electricity company faced the angry denunciation of the people.

Inside the walled grounds of a Catholic mission, Paiakan had also succeeded in building a native village to accommodate indigenous tribes while in Altamira. We were invited to visit. When we arrived, there was a strange mob scene up ahead under the trees. I could hardly make out what seemed to be a pack of journalists, microphones on poles, cameras, and tape recorders all jamming in for a better view—but of what?

A former British schoolteacher named Gordon Sumner, now known as Sting, was explaining why the dam should not be allowed. A Belgian filmmaker had been his introduction to the Kaiapo. Sting had decided to champion the cause of the rainforest and work with the Kaiapo to do it. Uncomfortably, I realized I had made a promise involving Sting. I had had a bizarre phone call a few weeks earlier from an environmental activist in Tokyo. He wanted me to contact Sting to ask him to play a concert in Japan. He felt sure that if Sting came to Japan, the issue of rainforest logging and the wasteful use of such wood in construction would grab public attention. I had been nonplussed. I explained that I did not know Sting and did not know anyone who did. The fellow had been adamant gaining my pledge that if ever I should run into Sting, I would deliver his message. It was an easy promise to make. There wasn't a chance in a million that I would ever meet Sting.[8]

As the Kaiapo danced with low rhythmic undercurrents of their haunting singing, I found myself standing next to Sting. It was eerily easy to chat to him about playing Tokyo. He assured me that he was planning to do a benefit concert in Japan already. I mentioned that I was part of a group of Canadians who had raised money for this event who had come to support it, including Gordon Lightfoot.

. Sting suddenly paid a lot more attention to me. "You mean Gordon Lightfoot is here?" I confirmed that indeed he was. "You mean he is here in Altamira?"

I replied, "He's here in this village under those trees over there."

Sting was amazed, he offered that it would mean so much to him to meet Lightfoot, that he had listened to him as a teenager and that his music had had a huge influence on him. But, Sting, being a bit stuck in place on what was an impromptu viewing stand, asked, "Could you ask him to come over here?" No problem.

Well, it was a bit of a problem. Lightfoot, as I knew by then, hated fuss. He is basically shy. So, I wandered over and explained that I had met someone who was a huge fan of his, and who hoped to meet him. He is also incredibly kind. The thought of meeting a star-struck fan in the Amazon presented no problem. As we got closer to the mob scene, I ventured gently, "Actually, the person who really wants to meet you is named Sting." I could feel his body tense.

He stopped in his tracks. "Look, Liz.[9] Is this going to be some sort of *thing*?" The word "thing" conjured a very clear picture of an embarrassing hassle.

I assured him there was no "thing"; that it simply would mean a lot to Sting to meet him. So we kept walking. I caught Sting's eye through the crowd and he stepped out of the circle. I introduced them and watched as both beautiful and talented men lit up in each other's presence. Afterwards, Lightfoot was thrilled. "We got the ball rolling in Canada," he said, "and now I've passed the ball to Sting."

The wire services of the world carried photos of Sting in the Amazon and carried news of the threat to indigenous people and the forest creatures from the proposed dam. Back in Canada, we kept up the pressure. The Canadian governor at the World Bank pledged to oppose the dam.

The World Bank board of governors voted not to fund the dam, but converted a loan to Brazil to PlanaFlora, to help protect the forest. The government of Brazil announced it would not build a dam on the Xingu. Paiakan had other trials ahead. Being a prominent indigenous organizer in Brazil is not easy. But he lives with a growing family in Aucre, and has now welcomed a grandchild who can grow up on the banks of the Xingu, flowing free.

LESSONS LEARNED IN CHOOSING YOUR GOAL:

1. Choose the goal that the issue demands. In environmental campaigns, do what the planet needs.
2. No compromises.
3. Be clear in your goal.
4. Never, ever, give up.
5. Expect your victory. See your victory.
6. Seize every opportunity.
7. Crying on the phone gets results (see fundraising).
8. Support each other.
9. Be creative.
10. Make your own miracles. If you don't believe in miracles, you are not facing facts.

Chapter 4

ESSENTIAL ELEMENTS OF YOUR CAMPAIGN
STEP BY STEP

EVERY CAMPAIGN HAS A NUMBER of key elements. Each one takes careful planning and each works to reinforce the others. As you read in chapter 1, organizing for change is about putting a case together, getting the word out, persuading the public that your cause has merit and finding ways to translate that public support into pressure on governments.

Take them step by step:

1) putting a case together = solid research;
2) getting the word out = media campaign;
3) persuading the public that your cause has merit = public mobilization;
4) pressure on governments = lobbying.

Each of these elements is essential. Each has its own moment and builds on the previous step. None of these efforts is so discreet and finite that it doesn't spill over into the other. You cannot get the word out unless you have done your homework; you cannot get the serious attention of politicians if you have not demonstrated that your concerns resonate with the public, and once you get the attention of politicians, your media credibility also increases, increasing you public profile and ability to mobilize the public. The momentum keeps building.

All of it needs some funding from somewhere. It may be your own bank account for a while. The adage "you have to spend money to make money" applies in campaigning. No one will write a cheque for a proposed campaign from a group that has no track record.

SOLID RESEARCH

Think of your campaign like a pyramid of effort. The base must be solid. Your base is research. You must have your facts straight.

Find out everything you can about the issue. If an ecosystem is threatened, know that ecosystem. How many species are there? Are there rare or threatened species? What are the eco-system functions and services? Do people rely on that wetland for their water supply? How much carbon is stored in that soil? Do existing jobs depend on that healthy ecosystem? If you are working to stop use of a chemical or pesticide, what are its effects? What has been studied? Are there health risks to people? To pets?

I am a child of the pre–World Wide Web generation. I know the Web is out there and an amazing research tool. I realize the advice I will give you may be an age-related mind-set, but I still think your best research tool is the telephone. Once you have found the name of a scientist working on the issue, pick up the phone. Ask him for his help. Explain your issue.

A WORD ABOUT SOURCES

Not all information is equally valid. Not all sources are of equivalent weight. The most reliable sources are those that have been subjected to rigorous peer review. Not all peer-reviewed journals are equally prestigious. The most well-respected scientific journals have instant credibility. Medical research published in the *Lancet* (the British medical journal) or the *New England Journal of Medicine* will be immediately respected. For scientific research and observations of ecological decline, trusted journals are *Nature* and *Science*. Be very wary of information found on the Internet unless it is cited from a reliable peer-reviewed source. Do not base your case on stories in the newspaper. Go to the source. Dig for solid research.

The concerns expressed by eminent people are very useful and have credibility. Scientists who have received the Nobel Prize, or who have chaired key committees, or conducted decades of research are all important sources.

Other generally reliable sources in your campaign will be those from government and industry (government and industry data may be incorrect, but no one can accuse your group of using biased information sources).

DO YOUR HOMEWORK

Collect the hard copy, peer-reviewed studies published in scientific journals on the subject. Read them. Understand them. Work on pronouncing the chemical names or technical terms perfectly and effortlessly. (I used to work over the pesticide names the government planned to spray over Cape Breton Island. The chemical was an organophosphate called fenitrothion. It was a cholinesterase inhibitor. Take it again from the top: OR-GAN-O-FOS-FATE...FEN-I-TRO-THION...COLIN-ESTER-ASE inhibitor. When I could deal with chemical names and the spray proponents tripped over them, the anti-spray movement gained credibility. President Dwight Eisenhower could not say "nuclear"; it came out "nu-cu-lar." Bush cannot even pronounce "Kyoto.")

Ask for help in coming to a clear understanding of the issue so that you can decode the scientific jargon for the layman, without doing damage to the concepts.

Never exaggerate.

If you make a mistake, admit it and correct it immediately. Credibility is essential for a public interest group. Once a reporter or politician thinks your information is unreliable, you have lost the battle. Check and double-check.

Nova Scotia anti-uranium activist Donna Smyth once developed and produced a CBC Radio *Ideas* series on the "Rise of the Citizen Scientist." The program detailed how, over and over again, citizens have had to master complex subjects to protect their health and the environment.

It can be intimidating to debate people who have doctorates in the subject. There can be a sense of inadequacy. Never forget that in a democracy, no issue should be left to the so-called experts. In any event, most issues are too complex for today's experts. They are specialists. Most issues require an interdisciplinary holistic view. Most environmental issues involve a wide range of disciplines—biologists, entomologists, soil scientists, hydrologists, toxicologists, economists, epidemiologists. On top of that mix, most issues also involve an element of scientific uncertainty. In any event, the questions relate to public policy. Nuclear engineers are in no position to determine the most economic energy source for our future. They are hopelessly biased in only one direction. In a democracy no issue can be viewed as too complicated or technical for the average person to grasp. Politicians, after all, rarely have any more scientific background than the average citizen. Often they have less. David Suzuki has described the average politician as a "scientific ignoramus."

BE PREPARED.

You may not be an expert, but you can read. Make a habit of collecting quotes from unassailable expert sources. (Always make note of the source.) If you can, commit them to memory. If not, carry a few index cards with the quote, the expert and the source. If your level of knowledge is questioned, do not be defensive or apologetic. "I may not be an expert, but I can read. Dr. So-and-So, Nobel laureate and leading expert has said...."

Just as war is too important to be left to the generals, key questions of our survival are too important to be left to the "experts." The role of the citizen scientist is as critical as the citizen activist.

Whatever the issue, make sure you have made a good-faith effort to really understand the other side. What are their key arguments? Really question and examine their case. Have they exaggerated economic impacts? Can you demonstrate that their numbers do not add up? Check their references. Are they credible? (I took apart the book *Skeptical Environmentalist* by Bjorn Lomborg by checking his footnotes. There were phantom notes that led nowhere; "personal communication" that provided weak references for important points; and allegations based on a paper, unpublished and never peer reviewed, once on a Web site and now removed.)

Ask to meet with the industry proponents. Find out directly from them as much as you can about the proposal. Maybe you can open a channel for dialogue.

Do not assume the industry/government/pro-industry lobbyists have actually done their homework. Subject their case to a fine-toothed comb. Follow the money. Who is funding the project? Are subsidies involved? Government grants? Why is an environmentally inappropriate project getting taxpayers' support?

My father, trained as an accountant, demonstrated the enormous value of a thorough review of the opposition's case during the budworm-spray campaign. After we prevented spraying in 1976 through a cabinet decision responding to evidence of a health risk, the following year the pulp company fought back ferociously. The CEO of Stora Kopparberg flew to Nova Scotia from Sweden. He threatened that if the government did not conduct a full-scale aerial assault on Cape Breton's forests, he would close the mill and put two thousand people out of work. He ominously told the suppertime television news, in thickly accented English, "Nova Scotia iz sick. It must take ze medicine."

In support of this chilling threat, the company released a massive report, purporting to make the case that forest mortality from the insect infestation would be so extensive that the pulp mill would be forced to close. Essentially, the company claimed it would run out of trees and the mill jobs would be gone in a matter of five years. While the rest of our committee was researching and writing fact sheets on the environmental and health risks of the chemicals, my father decided to read the industry report.

When he called me over late one night ("Elizabeth, I have something rather interesting to show you..."), I remember feeling just as I had in grade school when he tried to help me with my math homework. I was sure it was a waste of time, but I sat down and tried to at least appear attentive as he went through the report. He groused about how badly prepared it was. How the numbers in the text and the graphs did not agree. How it all appeared to have been thrown together at the last minute. My eyes glazed over. I may have dozed off. What woke me was his conclusion. Once he pulled together the key facts from Stora's own report, it was evident that, even with no spraying and the worst-case predicted forest mortality, the mill would have more than enough wood for the next forty years—based on the company's own data.

The accounting review of the Stora business case demolished the company's credibility with several cabinet ministers. Stora had to backtrack. It tried to invent new numbers. The job–blackmail argument was revealed for what it was: an empty threat.

Never assume the other side's case will hold water. Look for the holes.

ACCESS TO INFORMATION

You may have to use the Access to Information Act at the federal or provincial level to get some key facts to the light of day. If you hit pay dirt, you'll find the media is very receptive to stories that have a whiff of corruption or undue industrial influence in public affairs.

In most jurisdictions in the United States and Canada, there are laws to ensure citizen access to information. Although in some places, Freedom of Information systems can seem more like Freedom *from* Information, these access regimes can deliver valuable information. Follow the stated procedure to request the information, pay whatever fees are required and wait. And wait. It can take months, so file your information request as soon as you can. Ask for help from an established group that has been through the hoops. It can save you from making mistakes and losing precious time.

A WORD ON BROWN ENVELOPES

Once your issue is in the news and you are identified as a citizen organizer, you may find that sympathetic people within government or industry will send you information anonymously. These packages are usually just referred to as "brown envelopes." We got one once with details of the CANDU "sale" to China, and Canada's financial commitment of $1.5 billion in loan guarantees to cinch the deal. The envelope (brown, of course) had a fictitious Chinese restaurant as the return address. (I would love to thank the civil servant who risked their job to send us that information, but I don't know who it was.)

The information can be damaging to the government. Sometimes it is clearly *not* intended for public review. Be very careful to protect the identity of any source. If you suspect you know who sent you the information, make no effort to confirm it. If you think releasing the information from your group will make the source too easily spotted, ask another group to pass it along to a reporter. Whistle-blowers do not have adequate protection. Cover your trail, but get the information out into the public domain.

I have had "lucky breaks" over the years from a variety of leaks. Back in 1977, one Stora employee found evidence in the company files that a supposedly objective film documentary—attacking the government's decision not to spray for the second year in a row—had been funded by the company. The "documentary" had been aired on CBC TV and treated as solid and impartial. In fact, it was really paid propaganda for the pulp company. As unbelievable a coincidence as it was, I received a copy of the financial commitment on Stora letterhead the afternoon I was to debate the filmmaker on the CBC TV evening news. This was my first-ever televised debate. I was twenty-three. The filmmaker was a respected senior journalist. Shaking like a leaf, I remember pressing my feet firmly against the rung of the stool on which I was perched to avoid visible quaking. In the debate I revealed that the documentary was really an infomercial. The sparks flew. Denials ensued. But I was holding the evidence in my hand. I never knew who sent it. The media response was astonishing. The filmmaker was denounced. Editorials supported the anti-spray cause. Nothing works in the media like a leaked document.

At Sierra Club of Canada, we've received copies of briefings to cabinet in brown envelopes, results of toxic chemical testing not included in final reports, and even documents so secret that photocopying them would break federal law. The system is full of people of conscience. When something really stinks, they don't mind taking the lid off the garbage. As veteran U.S. journalist Helen Thomas, a quintessential member of the White House press corps says, "Don't give up. There's always a leak. There's always someone who's trying to save the country." (There is also always someone trying to save the planet.)

There is no better way to get reporters interested in your issue than a leaked document. (Some politicians have figured this out and leak documents about their own upcoming releases to enhance media interest.)

CREATE A PATH FOR ANY POLITICIAN TO THE RIGHT ANSWER: GIVE THEM THE ANSWER!

In addition to making your case on health-, environmental- and science-based grounds, think about the socio-economic implications. Be sure to have a credible alternative. ("We are not just against something. We are *for* something better!") Figure out what your proposal will cost. Ideally it should create more jobs than the proposal to which you object. Most often, environmentally sound proposals are better job-creators than destructive ones. The reason is simple: most damaging projects (mega-projects of all kinds) tend to be capital-intensive (meaning they cost a lot of money), while involving as little labour as possible. Environmentally sound and sustainable approaches are more labour-intensive and less capital-intensive.

PUTTING YOUR CASE TOGETHER

It is very helpful to write your own report on the issue early in the campaign. Get all the facts in one place, well-referenced. State your case and develop your alternative solution. You will find such a background document indispensable for new volunteers, interested media, and eventually decision-makers. It does not need to be expertly graphically designed. You can write it on any typewriter or computer and photocopy it. In other words, you don't need fancy publishing. You just need the facts.

From that source document, you should boil down key points for a fact sheet. It should be kept to a length that can be printed on a single, double-sided, eight-by-eleven sheet of paper. With computer software for desktop publishing, these fact sheets can easily be made to look very professional. But that is a secondary goal. The main objective of your publications is to provide credible information to people who are seeking it. Be sure to put a contact name (preferably your organization's name) and a way of contacting the group. (phone, mail, or e-mail.)

Be prepared for the fact that an overwhelming case in your favour, by itself, will not carry the day. The most solid case in the world is not enough. Proving that the opponents' argument looks like Swiss cheese will mean nothing without an effective public campaign.

For many neophyte citizens' groups this realization can be enormously demoralizing. You have done you homework. It is dead obvious that the proposed housing development in the middle of a wetland is a disaster. The leading hydrologist says so. The best the developer can say is that, absent adequate studies, the development will be monitored and corrective actions taken later...when it will be *too late*.

Dr. Ursula Franklin, a wise woman, has said, "I used to believe that people in government were well-intentioned, but ill-informed. I believed that if I made a strong and clear case, the officials would be bound to change their view. But after years of frustration, I now believe that people in government are well-informed, but ill-intentioned."

This is likely too harsh, but it makes the point. To win this fight, you will need to do more than make an overwhelming, solid, scientifically irrefutable argument to government. You need to create public support and media scrutiny so strong that the politicians will not dare ignore your cause.

LESSONS LEARNED:

1. You need to dig for facts.
2. There are no stupid questions.
3. Contact experts directly.
4. Build a library of solid research.
5. Never exaggerate.
6. Correct any mistakes immediately.
7. Develop alternatives.
8. Check the proponent's case carefully. Any errors will damage their credibility.
9. Build a strong base.
10 Stand on it and raise hell.

Chapter 5

HOW TO GET YOUR ISSUE IN THE NEWS

HAVING AN IMPACT ON PUBLIC OPINION requires getting your story in front of the public. Billions of dollars are spent every day trying to mould public opinion. The average North American was hit by three thousand advertising messages a day in 1991, up from only 560 in 1971.[10]

Advertising has significantly affected our values. My grandparents' generation believed, "Waste not, want not" and, "A penny saved is a penny earned." Those Depression-era slogans have been replaced with "Shop 'til you drop." The change was accomplished through advertising.

Public interest groups will never have the kind of money required to change public opinion through paid advertisements. Lacking money, we have to rely on the news media to reach the public. This route is fraught with peril. Your issue can be misrepresented. You can (and will) be mis-quoted. Your complex and well-prepared case will be reduced to an over-simplified sound bite.

I actually knew of an environmental group that got so disgusted with the mistakes in media coverage of its issues that it stopped doing any news releases or media outreach. When the new executive director of the organization showed up, she was astounded as the outgoing head explained that he had no media list. "Those people always get things wrong." He had cornered the market on high factual standards—and zero effectiveness.

My first disillusioning experience with national media news occurred in Chicago, December 1967. My mother had brought me with her to a convention of Dissenting Democrats, hoping to support an anti-war can-didate from within the Democratic Party to challenge President Lyndon Johnson. On our way to Chicago, we had heard that Minnesota's Democratic senator, Eugene McCarthy, was prepared to take on a standing Democratic president. McCarthy was one of our heroes already for his strong stance against the war in Vietnam. We were thrilled to be among his first supporters. The mood at the convention was euphoric. Thousands of people from across the U.S. gathered to cheer the senator, who gave one of the most brilliant speeches I have ever heard. (I remember key witty lines to this day.) As we stood in the hall among other friends from Connecticut, a producer from the CBS national news came up to us. He enthused about what a pretty row of ladies we were—wearing lots of red, white, and blue. He shamelessly name-dropped. "You ladies have all heard of Mike Wallace?" Yes, of course! "Well, how would you like to be on national television with Mike Wallace?" Of course, we would! Our instructions were simple: Ignore Mike Wallace standing in front of us. We were the wallpaper. Just keep clapping and cheering and waving our signs and we'd be on the national news. Yahoo.

As we stood there, looking to the distance, cheering a speech that had already ended, we heard Wallace as he spoke to the American people: "The people who came here to Chicago were hoping their candidate would be Bobby Kennedy. They are disappointed. It is Eugene McCarthy. He is grey, dull..." At this point, we interrupted en masse. "No, that's not true." "We never hoped for Bobby Kennedy." "We love Gene McCarthy!" "CUT!"

We watched as they went to another group of colourful supporters elsewhere in the hall. We watched the producer prep them. Wallace took his mark. Thirty seconds into his spiel, the next group also broke out in disagreement. The far end of the hall, we saw them try again. No one seemed to agree with Wallace about what we thought.

That night in the hotel, we watched the CBS news with interest. There was Mike Wallace, sitting in the empty hall. No pretty ladies in red, white, and blue who would disagree with his pre-packaged analysis formed a backdrop. He was surrounded by empty chairs and wilting balloons. "The people who came here to Chicago were hoping their candidate would be Bobby Kennedy. They are disappointed. It is Eugene McCarthy. He is gray, dull..." I hate to admit it, but I was glad when a Chicago policeman punched him in the stomach eight months later at the "real" Chicago convention.

Noam Chomsky argues that ownership of the media is concentrated in fewer and fewer hands, leading to manipulation to influence the public to a view favourable to the economic interests of the owners. *Manufacturing Consent*, the film documentary on Chomsky and his views, is compelling.

It is certainly true in the United States in the era of Fox "news" and CNN. Getting your issue in the news in the U.S. is much harder, but still possible. It is far easier in Canada.

Nevertheless, the media will cover your story if you are persistent and give them good content. The leader of the Canadian New Democratic Party, Jack Layton, rejects arguments from those on the Left who believe there is no point in pitching stories to the mainstream media. "We must stop treating the media like the enemy," he said. "They might be owned by our enemies but the workers need a good story and we've got to help them tell ours."

For all its flaws, getting the news media to indirectly deliver your message is, like democracy, the worst system except for all the others. You do not have a choice if you want to win the campaign.

Your media campaign is essential. Once you have your facts straight and a case to take to the public—go for it!

BUILDING RELATIONSHIPS

We are back to the guiding principle. To build a relationship with local reporters you need to think about what they need. You need to empathize.

Most reporters do not have the luxury of specializing. They are expected to cover everything—politics, municipal government, health, disasters, crime, and tax policy. Increasingly, electronic news media, particularly in the United States, has moved to give priority coverage to the sensationalist. Murders and car crashes get top billing. The trend is exposed in Michael Moore's Oscar®-winning documentary *Bowling for Columbine*. Even though crime rates are actually going down, coverage of violent crime is increasing. Sadly, this trend is now evident in Canada. My dad now calls the CBC Halifax television news "The Murder Show." Ontario Minister Jim Bradley likes to tease reporters in the legislative press gallery. As they wait for a press conference, he'll taunt, "I hear a siren. You guys better run."

This situation is no fun for reporters. Those who want to cover important policy issues do not generally like being pulled off whatever they are doing for a dead body. There have also been significant cutbacks in both the public and private news media. Fewer reporters have to cover just as many stories. Or more.

Understanding the pressure reporters endure will help you get good coverage for your issue. Do not live under the illusion that there are a lot of Bob Woodwards and Carl Bernsteins out there; that all you have to do is give them a "hot tip" and they will dig for the facts. They do not have time.

Even Woodward and Bernstein were not Woodward and Bernstein. The facts of the Watergate break-in were deliberately ignored by the news media in the period of the 1972 election. Reporters, en masse, decided it would be a manifestation of their personal dislike of Richard Nixon to pay too much attention to what seemed like a trail from the Watergate burglars to the White House. Nevertheless, once Nixon was re-elected, there were a couple of reporters who changed the world named Woodward and Bernstein. But don't expect to find them working in your local paper.

Become media literate. Analyze how the shows are paced and plotted. You need to pay attention to the news around you and how it is covered to get good coverage yourself. Pay attention to news stories about issues similar to the one you are championing. Notice the byline: who wrote that story? Make a note and add them to your media list. Notice the style of different publications: some like a detailed in-depth approach; others want something sassy that skims the surface. Know the type of coverage each publication or program delivers and tailor your approach to each one's style and needs. This effort will vastly increase the likelihood you can get your issue in the news. Notice the timing of the quotes (sound bites) that make it to the evening news. Notice that television needs interesting visuals. A lot of people making statements will not work as well to get television cameras out as a demonstration. Watch the news. Listen to the radio reports. Read the newspapers. You will be better at getting news coverage if you become a news junkie yourself.

You need to help the reporter cover your story by thinking about the angle. What makes your issue newsworthy? Especially, what makes your concerns newsworthy more than once?

The following is a quickie list of approaches:

- Is there any element of misspent public funds? Are taxpayers' dollars being wasted?
- Can you find an unlikely ally or unexpected angle? "Dog bites man" is not a story. "Man bites dog," is.
- Can you enlist a celebrity in your cause?
- Is there a human interest angle?

The following story from California shows how reporters will pick up on a story if there is a personal element:

Sun, Aug. 28, 2005
CONTRA COSTA TIMES
Activist takes her cause personally
By John Geluardi
Two years ago, Sherry Padgett was a very private person. She had never spoken in public, knew very little about public process and even less about inorganic toxins.

A Danville resident and mother of two, Padgett had spent her career working as a financial officer. Nothing in her background would have predicted she would become an unrelenting advocate for the responsible cleanup of a contaminated eighty-five-acre property along south Richmond's waterfront that was chock full of what the EPA categorizes as some of the worst carcinogens.

Her work over the past two years has resulted in changes of city, county and state policy toward the cleanup of the Zeneca site, which had been on track for residential development. In addition, her discovery of government mismanagement of the site has been partially responsible for three state Assembly bills, according to state Assemblywoman Loni Hancock, D-Berkeley.

On Wednesday it will be announced that she has received the prestigious Jefferson Award for Public Service for her dedication and effectiveness at the local level. The awards are issued by the American Institute of Public Service, which was co-founded by Jacqueline Kennedy Onassis in 1972.

Assemblywoman Loni Hancock said Padgett had made some remarkable political achievements.

YOUR MEDIA CONTACT LIST

This is one of the first tasks of a new group. It is a great assignment for one person to pull it together. You need the names of all your target newspapers, (don't forget the community weeklies, and student-run university papers), all radio and TV stations (don't forget community radio and university radio stations), and freelance reporters with an interest in your issue. You need to collect the phone, fax, and e-mail addresses. At first, you may only have collected the news-desk information, but you will want to keep the list current and add to it over time. You will add the names of journalists and the names of specific producers of different current-affairs programming.

Remember that sending a single news release to a television station that has a morning news show, a suppertime news program and a mid-morning coffee show, means that only one of them will see the release. If you properly address each release to each different show, it will reach three shows and triple your chances of coverage on that station.

There are a number of types of announcements to the news media. We'll review them here in a descending order from the one you will use the most (the news release), through to the press conference, and then how to respond to media questions.

"JUST THE FACTS, MA'AM"

To get media coverage, do all of the reporters' homework for them. Your media releases should follow the five W's of all reporting: who, what, when, where, and why.

Write your news release just as you would like to see it in the newspaper. Many groups make the mistake of writing a news release as if it was a rousing speech; a diatribe. A press release is *not* a place for your manifesto. It is not a rant. It should be concise (economy of words is a virtue), well-written and informative.

All your releases should follow the same basic pattern:

1) Your heading should be "NEWS RELEASE" in big letters. If your group has stationery, or a logo, that should be at the top of the page in balance with the news release headline.
2) Indicate when the release is to be made public. Usually news releases are for immediate release, so write "FOR IMMEDIATE

RELEASE" in big letters at the top. Sometimes, you want to send out a release with a longer document. If you want to give reporters time to absorb the document, before the news hits the street, you can delay release by using the word "embargoed." Reporters will generally respect a notice on the release that it is "EMBARGOED UNTIL 10 A.M. SEPTEMBER 12." If your release is to be embargoed be very precise about the release time.

3) You need a catchy headline. It should serve as a hook to get reporters interested in your story. (Examples: "Local group slams illegal use of funds," or "Scientist urges action on toxic time bomb.")

4) Just before you get into the text, write the town or city from which the release is being issued.

5) In your first paragraph, set out the key facts. For instance:

> The Society to Save the Whole World today released the results of an independent, arm's length audit of the state's pollution enforcement record since the election of Governor I.M. Vile. The audit reveals that under Governor Vile's watch, prosecutions against polluters have dropped by 80 percent as against the previous administration.

6) Now that you have set the stage, use a quote. The quotes are where you an inject colour, memorable one-liners, zingers. You can make up the quote for someone else in your group, as long as they both agree to the quote and are happy to be available to the media for follow-up calls:

> "Frankly, we were shocked," said Dr. I.M. Good, author of the report. "We had heard anecdotally that pollution prosecutions had dropped, but the empirical data showed a far more dramatic trend than we expected."

7) Throw in more information, more detailed background:

> The research demonstrates that in 2002 there were 400 pollution offences reported, of which 380 resulted in prosecutions, with 319 convictions. In 2003, there were 490 citizen complaints, of which 80 resulted in prosecutions with 78 convictions.

8) Another quote carries the story forward:

> "We verified with the monitoring done by the university that water pollution has actually increased, so the drop off in prosecutions is not because there is less pollution," said Kermit Green, spokesperson for

The Society We Want (TSWW). "We hate to think that prosecutions for breaking the laws that protect our children's health depend on who donated to Governor Vile's campaign."

9) Closing paragraph, more information:

Last month it was reported that Heavy Industry R Us (HIRU) was the largest campaign contributor to Elect Vile. In 2002, of the 380 prosecutions, 180 were against HIRU or its subsidiaries. In 2003, there have been no prosecutions against HIRU.

10) It is a journalistic tradition to end a release with "–30–." This convention lets a reporter know that there is no more to the release. If your release is more than one page, write "more" at the bottom of the first page.

11) Following the "–30–," list under "Contact" the names and phone numbers of people quoted in the release and your group's office number (if you have one). Be sure that the people quoted will be at the number listed, prepared, and available to talk to reporters during the day of the release.

That's all there is to it. Your release should ideally run no more than a single side of an eight-by-eleven piece of paper. It is not a serious offence to run to a page and a half, but two pages is too long. You can also release a "backgrounder" document with your release for facts and figures you really want the reporters to have and keep in their files.

Send your news release by fax or e-mail. Life has gotten a lot easier for activists with e-mail. When I started, we did not yet have fax machines, but I could get a release written in rural Cape Breton to every news outlet in Nova Scotia, by phoning it in to the Canadian Press in Halifax. Wire services like Canadian Press, and in the U.S., Reuters and Associated Press, work by having a group of reporters writing stories, which are then syndicated, to various newspapers that pay for the service.

THE PRESS CONFERENCE

The news conference is a larger commitment of time and energy for you and for the reporters you are hoping will attend. Use news conferences sparingly. Unless you have a good reason to seek a news conference, use a news release. Good reasons for news conferences include:

- A famous, prestigious or hugely knowledgeable person is endorsing your cause. The media are more likely to attend if the person is from another province, state or better yet, a different country. (As Jesus noted, it is hard to be a prophet—or get media attention—in your hometown.)
- A significant announcement, such as going to court;
- Releasing a major study;
- Announcing a coalition effort where you gather an impressive array of forces that had not been joined before.

To hold a successful news conference, follow the cardinal rule: empathize. If you make it easy for reporters to attend, they will be more likely to get there.

What is the most convenient place to hold a news conference? We are awfully lucky at the Sierra Club of Canada National office, as the Parliamentary Press Gallery maintains a very professional news studio, available free of charge. It is in Centre Block on Parliament Hill and has closed-circuit television to the offices of every member of Parliament and to the reporters' working offices several floors above. (I quite like that the room on the third floor is labelled with a lovely brass engraving reading "The Hot Room.") There are similar facilities in most capital cities connected with the legislature. If such a facility is not available in your community, be sure to pick a place that is central and well-known. A church basement may be free, but if reporters think it is too far out of the way, they are less likely to get to your conference. A downtown hotel is a good choice. Serve coffee.

What time suits the reporters' schedules? Shoot for a news conference before noon to allow maximum time for the conference to be covered and for reporters to write their story. Reporters have filing deadlines. Don't expect them to drop everything screaming, "Stop the presses!" to squeeze in your news item.

Think about what governments do when they announce something unpopular. The announcement is at 5 PM on a Friday before a holiday weekend. Or it gets announced between Christmas and New Year's. Do the opposite. The best days for news conferences are Tuesday, Wednesday and Thursday.

THE INVITATION

To announce that you will be holding a news conference, prepare a notice to media (sometimes called a media advisory). This is an invitation. It is not a news release, but like a news release, it needs a hook. The content of your notice to media should be a teaser. You need to hint at what you will be releasing, but not spill the beans. Don't scoop yourself by giving out your actual announcement before the news conference.

Your notice to media should start with the words "NOTICE TO MEDIA" and then your catchy headline: "Group to disclose evidence of on-going cover-up," or "Nobel laureate to confirm results of citizens' group's study."

In very clear fashion set out the time and location of your event:

Time: 10 AM
Date: Thursday, March 4
Location: Press Theatre, Ohio Legislature, Room 200B.

Then you should list the speakers who will participate. In countries with media operating in more than one language, it is good to note which of your speakers will be making statements in French or Spanish.

Ideally, you should send out your invitation several days ahead of the press conference. The week before allows too much time for your news conference to be forgotten. The day before is too last minute for assignment editors. If your news conference is on Tuesday, a notice to media on Friday is perfect.

Now that the announcement has been sent out, you need to make phone calls as reminders to the key news outlets. If your news conference is Tuesday and your Notice to Media was faxed on Friday, then Monday is a perfect time to make follow-up calls. These calls are not merely static reminders. You should be prepared to pitch your event. Really urge the assignment editor to send a reporter. Convince the reporter that attending the event will give her a really good story.

THE EVENT ITSELF

Running a good news conference requires a brisk professionalism for which reporters will thank you.

Be prepared. Have a news release that summarizes everything that will be announced. Include the names and affiliations of every speaker, properly spelled and with phone numbers for follow-up questions. Ideally, in Canada, have a French-language news release as well as an English one.

Start on time.

Choose speakers who are articulate. Avoid mumblers, unless your famous person happens to be one. Avoid the temptation to ramble on and on about your issue. Keep your opening statements to no more than fifteen minutes, *in total*. This means you need to keep the number of speakers to no more than five, each taking up three minutes. It is better to have fewer speakers, but other experts can be present and identified. The reporters are there to ask questions; they do not just want to take notes on your long-winded discourse. Make sure you allow time for them to ask the questions. Be sure to keep the whole conference to about half an hour.

VISUALS

A news conference has an unfortunate tendency to be a series of "talking heads" on the evening news. This is boring for television news producers. Think about ways to spice it up.

Some amazingly lame efforts at visuals are much appreciated. When we had thousands of names on petitions to save Jim Campbell's Barrens, we invited the premier to the news conference, placed his name on an empty chair and ceremoniously dropped the stack from about a foot up. As a key organizer handed the petitions to members of opposition parties, the television cameras moved in for a close-up of the petitions dropping on the premier's empty chair. The stack of petitions delivered a satisfying "thump," which made it onto the evening news. When we had postcards from over eighty thousand Canadians asking for strong action to be taken at the negotiations in Kyoto, Japan (December 1997), we brought the postcards in cloth bags to the news conference and dumped them into a growing pile with news cameras rolling. I have always loved the final scene in *Miracle on 34th Street* as the letters to Santa Claus cascade on the judge's desk. This was our *Miracle on 34th Street* moment. A few maps and a pointer will also help. For a press conference about the amount of toxic waste leaching from a landfill toward a housing development in Ottawa, we made a map on Bristol board. The map included a bar graph with thick red lines made of red crepe paper showing the amount from various readings and international standards. The readings from the Ottawa site were literally off the charts. To demonstrate this, as we described the issue, one of our youth interns started unrolling the yards and yards of red crepe paper rolled up behind the map. It extended across the room and provided a nice visual for the evening news. Virtually anything will liven up a group of images of people talking!

Another very smart approach is to provide the news media with video footage suitable for broadcast. The media term for this is "B-roll." If you are trying to save somewhere beautiful and remote, get a filmmaker or journalism student to take some good images for you. Edit them to about one and a half minutes. Do not include anyone talking over the images. Let the forest or wetland speak for itself.

Dr. Ransom Myers of Dalhousie University released a major study in May 2003 on the declining state of fish populations all around the world. The study, co-authored with Dr. Barry Worm, was featured on the front cover of *Nature* magazine, one of the most prestigious scientific journals in the world. The study was front page news in the *New York Times*, and Myers was interviewed on nearly every major television news broadcast around the world: CNN, ABC, CBS, CBC, CTV, Spanish TV, and so on. I asked him how he had done it. That kind of news attention for an environmental story in a scientific journal does not happen without some pretty significant effort. Sure enough, he had received a grant for his research and used a large chunk of it on media relations. Having studied how the news media worked, he decided, "I want to do it like NASA does it—graphics, animation, visuals."

Once the research paper was accepted for publication by *Nature*, several people had worked for months pitching the story to major news outlets. Myers hired a submersible and a filmmaker to shoot new images of ocean life, ideal for television news. The B-roll footage, prepared on beta, was sent to major news organizations with prepared interviews of Myers. The interview segments, separate from the ocean-life bits, were tailored to the various lengths and styles of programming from news stations around the world. Cool animation was available on his Web site and could be downloaded for broadcast. Very sophisticated stuff. Myers is a rare commodity: a scientist who knows how to communicate.

MEDIA BRIEFINGS

Now and then it is a good idea to hold an in-depth information briefing for the media. This is a hybrid. It is more of a seminar than a press conference. A media briefing makes sense in advance of large and complex negotiations, such as on the climate change issue, or on trade and environment questions. Reporters who are being thrown in at the deep end, covering an issue about which they do not have a lot of background, are grateful for a session where they can get a primer on what to expect, key issues, and the factual background to the story. The media briefing is organized the same way as a press conference, (issue a "notice to media" as your invitation), but the session is held in a more informal atmosphere, usually around a table, instead of theatre-style, and the briefing will last longer than a press conference. Where a press conference is unlikely to run for more than a half-hour, a media briefing will last an hour or two.

For a briefing session, you should prepare a solid media kit. Key facts should be included. If the briefing is in advance of negotiations, a chronology of the previous negotiations and history of the organization (WTO, Conference of the Parties of various UN treaties) is very helpful. Graphics, charts and photographs in publishable form are great additions. If you have an expert on the topic participating, include his CV (curriculum vitae).

EDITORIAL BOARDS

Similar to a media briefing is the meeting with the editorial board. Every newspaper has an editorial board. Generally the board meets once a day to debate the latest news, consider the pros and cons of different issues, and develop the newspaper's editorial policy. You can ask to meet with the editorial board to explain your point of view on a key issue. It is always a good idea to bring an expert who can communicate clearly. You want to leave a lasting impression for having been reasonable and credible. These sessions involve a fair deal of verbal sparring. Expect the devil's advocate. Know that you are being tested. Do not take offense. This is more like a university debating club than a genuine expression of opinion. If you hold up well under fire, deliver solid responses and have your facts straight, you may help shift the newspaper's editorial stance.

DEMONSTRATIONS OR STUNTS

Sometimes you can get coverage for your issue by staging something specifically for the news media. A large demonstration is usually about much more than media coverage. It is an awareness building event; it is a way of influencing government.

However, smaller, symbolic events can be perfect for news coverage. A mock funeral, any event involving children (painting things, planting things, carrying signs), a candlelight vigil, a silent vigil, standing outside a public hearing with tape covering mouths in protest against a restrictive approach to public participation. Greenpeace has made the media stunt its stock-in-trade: hanging banners, climbing the CN Tower, displaying banners from suspension bridges. (I sometimes joke that I am not in Greenpeace because I am afraid of heights.) No matter whether or not you would run a campaign the same way, there is no arguing with success. The big, bold, audacious stunt gets media coverage every time.

The approach to symbolic protests and demonstrations is the same as for news conferences. Send out a notice to media or media advisory with the crucial information in advance.

And if you do all these things perfectly, you are guaranteed media coverage—*not*!

The reality is that in the news business, coverage is a lottery. Sometimes you will be lucky. It is a slow news day. Your half-baked press release, thrown out "on speculation" gains top billing on the evening news. Other times, your painstakingly prepared, newsworthy report is shut out by other late-breaking news.

I will never forget my first press conference in Toronto. It was actually my first trip to Toronto. I was living in Cape Breton and decided that a group of environmentalists should run in the upcoming federal election. It was January 1980. Prime Minister Joe Clark's Progressive Conservative minority government had fallen. I was watching television and saw Pierre Trudeau's first ad. No pun intended, but I saw red. It had no content about real issues. It was a negative attack ad. If a group of us ran for office and highlighted the need to protect the environment and shut down nuclear power, we could change the tenor of the debate to include some real issues. With that in mind, I started making phone calls. Before the deadline for filing as independent candidates, there were thirteen of us in six provinces, banded together under the banner of British economist E.F. Schumacher, and his best-selling book, *Small is Beautiful*. My new-found friends in Toronto decided they would organize a press conference to announce our quixotic effort.

It was a big deal. I flew to Toronto. We had a beautiful venue for the press conference, and to our amazement, the national television crews and reporters from the two major national networks attended. The major national newspaper reporters were there. The fabulous volunteer with lots of media experience who organized the press conference was euphoric. We went back to the apartment where I was billeted to watch our coverage. The CBC television news at 10 PM opened with the trustworthy face of Knowlton Nash. He began with a startling announcement: "Tonight we will be abandoning our usual format in order to concentrate on our lead story: Canadian Ambassador Ken Taylor has smuggled six Americans out of Iran…" Naturally I was happy six Americans had been smuggled out of Iran, but we had been shut out of virtually any coverage. There was no hope of getting coverage the next day, at least, certainly not for the same announcement.

I should have remembered this. My mother once worked for weeks on a press event wiped off the pages by Lana Turner's daughter fatally stabbing her mother's boyfriend. Celebrity and sensationalist coverage is not entirely new.

The flip side of the bad news that you may be blown out of the water by a late-breaking news development is that your group will benefit from a disproportionate amount of coverage (relative to the effort involved) on a slow news day. I experienced that effect not too long ago. It was a Friday in August and I was working in Cape Breton on issues relating to the health of Sydney residents near the Sydney Tar Ponds. The provincial medical officer had made yet another infuriating statement that the high cancer rates in Sydney had nothing to do with the toxic waste, the largest toxic waste site in the country. It took me about ten minutes to write a press release in which Sierra Club of Canada called for his removal as medical officer. I sent it out over our electronic media list, without much thought that it would make any splash. Goodness knows why, but the story went national. It was on the hourly national radio news. It made it all the way to the British Columbia newspapers. And, due to what must have been a news drought that weekend, it kept being covered over a period of three days. A slow news day will result in a lot more coverage than you could expect otherwise.

So the key is to know when there will be a slow news day. How can you predict when there will be a slow news day? You cannot.

So, is it hopeless?

No. Just as in real estate the top three desirables are location, location, location, the key to getting media coverage is volume, volume, volume. Since it is impossible to know when there will be a slow news day, your group should remember to issue news releases frequently. (Remember not to overdo press conferences, or reporters will get tired of being dragged to your events. Save those face-to-face events for significant developments.) A news release can respond to something a politician has said; it can re-emphasize findings from a report you released last month, but for which you received no coverage. The media is fickle. Getting coverage is a crap shoot. Like a lottery, if you want to increase your chances of winning, buy more tickets!

THE INTERVIEW

Often you will be asked to give a media interview. You may be terrified. Don't be. Unless you think you will not overcome a fear of being interviewed (in which case another member of your group should take on the task), you will do well if you prepare well.

The first step is to listen to the radio program you will be on, watch the TV show you will be on, read the newspaper the reporter works for in advance. Get a feel for the style and format of the particular media outlet. Be comfortable with the length of the interview. Notice the format. Do you hear the interviewer ask the question or do you just hear the answer? If you do not hear the question, then you know the format does not rely on the question at all. It is simply a way of getting you to say something. Does the person being interviewed get time to build an argument, or will you be restricted to a short sound bite?

Before you do the interview, you and your group should consider your main message. The message of your campaign is ideally one you design in the planning of the campaign strategy and stick to throughout. "Staying on message" is a current buzzword in communications. It is important to stay with the same theme. Frankly, I think it can be overdone. The public can tell when a politician is sticking to a line and they may tune out. I think environmentalists and other campaigners on social issues are more engaging and sound more natural when they speak from the heart. The key message must always be embedded in your communications. You need not always use precisely the same words.

Once you know the key message you want to convey, find ways to say it over and over again. If the question asked by an interviewer is not germane, do not get sucked into trying to address it. If the format means the question is never aired, just ignore it. If the listening audience hears the question, acknowledge the question, and move on: "That's an interesting question, but the key issue here is ..." Most interviewers are not actually interested in the question if it is not relevant to your key issue.

If your interview is one where you and the reporter will be seen or heard together, do use their first name. Radio hosts usually begin with a "Good morning, Ms. Wilson." Be sure to reply, "Good morning, Don." Acting like you belong on the airwaves and having the host acknowledge you is an immediate, subtle cue to the audience that you are credible. If you are given the option of going into the radio studio to do the interview, do it! One of the very subtle ways that some voices on air are more credible than others is the sound quality.

I figured this out when Peter Gzowski was hosting the national CBC morning program, *Morningside*. He had, sadly for us, become enamoured of Patrick Moore, the Greenpeace founder who had emerged as an industry lobbyist. Moore, dubbed "Eco-Judas" by the late (and wonderful) Bob Hunter, another Greenpeace founder, had already been interviewed by Gzowski. Moore had trotted out his usual nonsense ("A clear-cut is a temporary meadow"). Audience reaction had been very negative. Rather than bring an environmentalist into the studio to chat with Gzowski about the other side of the issue, CBC was bringing Moore back into the studio to respond to his critics. CBC had lined up three very well-informed folks— one in Victoria, one in Edmonton, and one in Vancouver to take him on.

The three environmental voices were on their home phones. Moore was in a CBC studio and had an immediate advantage. A radio station's studio microphones allow for modulation and inflections lost on telephones. The studio voice has the ring of authority. Moore sounded like the voice of God. My friends on telephone lines sounded like whining cranks over the static. If you are given the option and are near a studio, go into the studio, even if it's 6 AM. Go into the studio!

Be polite. Be sincere. Smile at the beginning and again at the end (especially for TV, although a private smile of relief at home after a radio interview is appropriate).

One of the hardest ways to be interviewed is what is called a "double-ender." This only applies to television and is used when the station wants you to be interviewed, but not in the same studio as the person asking the questions. No doubt you have seen people in double-ender situations. They are a "head in a box," sometimes several to a screen, all in different places, all talking to the same questioner, often the national news anchor in Toronto.

Here's what it feels like for the head in the box. You are in a chair, generally with no other human in the small room with you. The technician has stuck a wire in your ear so you can hear everyone else. There will be a volume control coming down the wire behind your back and near your hand. You will be facing a camera, but the cameraman is generally in another room. You will not see any of the other people; that's for the viewers at home. Before the interview starts make sure you can really hear well through the do-hicky thing in your ear (that's the technical name). They will test it. Don't be nice about it if you can only partially hear. Make sure the sound quality is very good. Things move fast in double-enders and if you cannot hear the questions properly, it gets scary fast. Keep eye contact, as though there is a real person hiding in the camera. The camera lens should be your focus at all times. Do not let your eyes wander. It is natural, if alone in a room and asked a question to look up slightly and ponder your response. Do this in a double ender, and you'll look like an escapee from a loony-bin. Sit up straight, never slouch. Look confident and professional at all times. Don't scratch. Don't fidget. The camera is on you and you may be in screen even when someone else is talking. For that reason, if it is a debate, you can raise eyebrows in disbelief. You can convey by your facial expression that what the other person is saying is getting under your skin. To keep the evening news visually interesting, once you start making a few skeptical faces, the screen will start showing your reaction. This can be very effective communication!

You will find that there is no media training as effective as just doing it. The more interviews you do, the more comfortable you will be. It is a good idea to tape yourself and be a Monday-morning quarterback. How could you have improved? Can you practice to avoid the time wasting "umms" and "ahhs"? Time on-air is very valuable. Use every second to persuade your audience.

OFF THE RECORD

There is no such thing as "off the record." Anything you say to a reporter can end up in public. "Off the record" can mean that it ends up in print without you being cited as the source. You will be seen as a background source. You were not speaking "*on* the record," but you were talking to a reporter. Suppose you have a press conference and then adjourn to the local pub where you end up sitting with a reporter drinking beer. A red neon sign should be flashing: DANGER! Anything you say to a reporter any time could end up in the media. You may end up being quoted. If you want to be really certain something you know does not end up in the newspaper, there is one simple rule: *do not tell a reporter.*

I'll never forget having a leisurely brunch with a good friend visiting Ottawa. A friend of hers was a reporter writing a profile of me. (Another danger sign: any story about an individual, instead of being about your issue, is hazardous.) They had arranged to have him join us near the end of the brunch and start the interview from there. Here is where I made a huge mistake. I didn't think my end of brunch conversation with our mutual friend was part of the interview. It had been her birthday recently and I had bought her a very pretty necklace with a crystal. We started talking about crystals. I had a vague sense that crystals were supposed to either channel or store energy. I shared what I thought people who believed in crystals actually believed about them. I gave her the necklace because it was pretty. You, no doubt, can imagine what happened. I was portrayed as some sort of fanatic over crystals. And the story went down hill from there. Based on that, another environmental reporter wrote a book about the Canadian environmental movement in which I ended up described as "into the occult." Good grief. Me, a practicing Anglican! Lesson learned.

You can have a friend who is a reporter, but you can never trust that your reporter/friend to be such a good friend that things you say may not end up in print.

BE HELPFUL

As you embark on a media strategy, you will start knowing reporters. And they will know you. You may get phone calls from reporters seeking your help. Your future opportunities for good media coverage increase enormously if you see yourself as an assistant to the reporter. If you get a call, remember the reporter is working to a deadline. If the reporter asks you a question on a subject about which you know nothing, do not simply decline to be interviewed. Throw yourself into helping her out in the next ten minutes. Say, "I am not the right person to talk to about that, but if you give me a few minutes, I can get back to you with the right contact." Chances are that with a few phone calls to other groups or experts, you can turn up the person who meets the reporter's immediate need. Ideally, you should be able to call the reporter back and say, "I've just spoken with Dr. Rivers. He is expecting your call and is available right now. Here is his number."

You can imagine what will happen after you have done this a few times. Your phone number moves to the top of the reporter's Rolodex. Calling your group becomes the first step in preparing any story relating to the issue on which you are working. As a matter of ethical practice, you should not give interviews about subjects on which your group is not working. (There are a number of groups that do that [media hogs] and it is frowned upon, especially by the group actually doing the work!) Conversely, if you call a group and line them up for a media interview, they will be grateful, and the reporter will be happy. You are building relationships. Providing good service to media delivers better coverage for your issue, as well as gratitude from the reporter and a colleague in another organization.

Like everything else in campaigning, getting good media coverage is hard work. Nevertheless, it is essential and can be very effective.

LESSONS LEARNED

1) Do not be intimidated. You can do this!
2) Reporters are overworked and rarely are able to specialize. Be helpful.
3) Be accurate.
4) Do *not* go "off the record."
5) Write frequent, crisp, and newsworthy press releases.
6) Think about creating good visuals to increase television coverage.
7) Be of service to reporters. *Always return a reporter's phone message immediately,* (if not sooner)!
8) Do their work for them. Do as much as you can to anticipate their needs.
9) Stay on message.
10) Become media literate. If you never watch the TV news, do not expect to be brilliant at getting your issue out there.

Chapter 6

VOX POPULI
GETTING YOUR MESSAGE OUT DIRECTLY

GETTING THE NEWS MEDIA TO come to you is only one way to get your message out.

·There are a number of absolutely free ways to get your campaign in the public eye. A short list of free and accessible media include letters to the editor, opinion pieces, open-line radio and television shows, public service announcements (PSAs), and Internet "indie" media. Be sure to include these approaches in any campaign plan. They have the added benefit of meeting some of your organizational goals in keeping everyone involved.

As well, you can pay for the space—on-air or in the pages of the newspaper. Generally, most groups do not have the kind of money it takes to make any impact with paid advertising, but it can sometimes be effective.

LETTERS TO THE EDITOR

The most-read section of every newspaper is the letters-to-the-editor page. People love reading what members of their community think about current issues. People enjoy a letter that gives them a laugh; that is witty and brief.

There are a number of reasons to write letters to the editor and you have three major intended audiences:

1) The readers of the newspaper. You want to persuade more people of the rightness of your cause. You want to expose more people to key facts.
2) The political decision-makers. Federal ministers have a clipping service that ensures every letter to the editor from a major daily paper related to their portfolio is on the minister's desk first thing every morning.

3) The newspaper itself. The newspaper editorial board and assignment editors are interested in what issues interest their readers. Even if your letter isn't published, the letter may influence the paper to devote more space and attention to issues you care about.

TIPS TO GET YOUR LETTERS PUBLISHED:

- Relate your letter to a recent article in that newspaper. Mention the article and date it appeared.
- Send your letter the same day as the story you're commenting on appeared.
- Look carefully through each day's newspapers to find articles that give you a hook.
- Keep your letter brief. When the letters page advises that letters must be kept to two hundred words, they mean it.
- Be sure to include your address, work and home phone numbers, and e-mail address. Many newspapers will check with you to verify that you really sent the letter. They need to know how to reach you.
- Send the letter to only one newspaper. Editors dislike seeing an identical letter to one they have published in another paper. Use the same template, but modify each letter for each paper.
- Use humour. Include a zinger. You are more likely to be published if you make your point with wit.
- Never send an anonymous letter.
- Don't be discouraged if your letter is not published. Try, try again.
- The secret to getting letters published is volume, volume, volume.

One of the ways you can use the talents of everyone in your group is to find someone willing to write lots of letters. The same person will not generally be published repeatedly, and you want to be sure lots of different names are associated with your cause. Match up the talented writer with the busy people who would happily sign a letter prepared for them.

Once Mark Twain mailed a letter he claimed he had written to the *New York Times* to one of his best friends, the rather stuffy William Dean Howells. The letter was an ungrammatical mess: "The goddam gov'ment has gone too far dis time." Twain's note to Howells said, "I have signed your name as I was sure it would carry more weight." (Mr. Clemens was a serious practical joker.)

Obviously, never submit anything in someone else's name without their full agreement to every syllable, and awareness of when the letter is being sent.

Increasingly, e-mail is used to get letters to the newspapers. If you do not use a computer, try to get your letter sent by fax the same day the article on which you are commenting appeared. The time between when the story you are writing about appears and when newspapers consider a letter to the editor topical is constantly shrinking. Thanks to enhanced technology, letters sent by "snail mail" (regular post) are likely to arrive well past the media's "best before" date. Your best bet is to send your letter to the paper on the same day the story prompting it appeared.

OPINION PIECES

Every newspaper has a section for opinion articles. The section is usually opposite the editorial page, and, as a result, such articles are often referred to as op-eds (*op*posite the *ed*itorial). Typically, the papers ask that such submissions be kept to about eight hundred words.

Such articles are one of the most effective ways to make your case. Unlike a media interview, you control exactly how your message appears. Your piece may be edited, but generally lightly, for grammar and syntax. The content is yours. While an eight-hundred-word article is not a treatise, you will be surprised how cogently you can develop your argument in that small space. The opinion piece also has the benefit of good profile in the paper. At the end of the piece, a one-liner describing you appears. You can often include the Web site address for your group in this space. Some newspapers even pay a small amount for publishing such articles.

To get an opinion piece published, it is best to contact the editor for the op-ed page and pitch your idea. It is best to have nailed down a willingness to publish before you write your article, especially for the larger daily papers. However, I have also had articles published when I sent them on spec.

The opinion page can also benefit from a tie-in to your celebrity efforts. If you have a prominent person supporting your campaign you can draft an article and ask if they would be willing to sign it. This reduces their workload in agreeing. Generally, people will not accept someone else's draft unchanged, but the time and effort required is substantially reduced when an op-ed piece is prepared for someone whose name adds clout.

I found it positively thrilling to call the *Globe and Mail* and ask if they would be interested in an opinion piece by Harrison Ford. The actor filmed *Mosquito Coast* in Belize and had become a fan of the area's rain-forests. A Canadian company, Fortis of Newfoundland, built a dam in a critical biodiversity hotspot on the Upper Macal River. While we were still trying to stop construction, Ford's article was sent to me through his agent, and I think he wrote every word himself. I never had an easier time securing a place in a major newspaper.

OPEN-LINE RADIO AND TV SHOWS

If there is an open-line show in your area, make a habit of listening and phone in with your concerns. Increasingly these shows have become combative and anti-environmental, but that is not universally the case. Even if the show's host is very challenging, getting on-air allows you to inject a different view. Many of these programs do not have an assigned topic for the day. They just want to hear what is on the minds of their listeners. Sometimes, there are opportunities to phone in and ask questions of experts or guests in the studio. Be prepared to call in and ask questions of anyone in your group to help them fill in the air time. Radio shows hate it when there is "dead air" on an open-line show. Keep it lively with lots of callers. Plan your strategy to cover points other callers have not made.

Back in the mid-1970s, I was on an open-line show in Cape Breton with Frank Reid, head of the county Woodlot Owners and Operators Association. We were both studio guests, invited to make the case against budworm spraying. I was about twenty-two years old and hadn't done much media at that stage. It did not make me feel any less nervous as I realized that the woman who had just phoned in was my mother. She was using some sort of accent to disguise the fact. She was speaking ungrammatically to fit her idea of the sort of person who phoned in to open-line radio programs. Frank made eye contact with me, clearly signaling that he too had realized my mother was our caller. The host had no idea. I was suppressing a growing hysteria. My mum was on a roll, talking about the threat of poison spraying. In her enthusiasm she seized on the example of Cesar Chavez and the grape workers who were directly sprayed in the fields. Somewhere between the time she spoke the name "Cesar" and before she uttered "Chavez," it occurred to her that the imaginary woman she was imitating would never have heard of the activist. It was all I could do from dissolving in laughter when she switched gears and told all of Cape Breton that Cesar Romero, the actor, had been poisoned by pesticides.

The key to making an impact through such open-line shows is to become familiar with the format and the host. Listen to the show for a few days before calling in. Find a way to fit in to the overall tone. Clearly this advice will not help you with Rush Limbaugh, but that doesn't mean you shouldn't even try going head to head with an appalling individual. People are listening and may be influenced. If you are ever dealing with a belligerent host, or debating a nasty individual, remember, never lose your cool. Staying polite, keeping your feet firmly planted on high ground, will be your best protection. Listeners will sympathize with you.

My first-ever televised interview was when I was in high school. A local call-in show wanted me to discuss the work of our high school ecology club. The host was famous for being a boor and a bully. I was sixteen and looked younger. He did not want me to fall apart and cry on-air, so before the show began, he took me aside and gave me great advice. "People watch this show because I make them mad. A lot of them hate me. So when I take you on, you come right back at me. The audience will be rooting for you."

He taunted me about everything. He took an apple, claimed it was sprayed with DDT and said he ate them all the time. I can still remember saying, "Well, that explains a lot." I had a ball being sarcastic and mean, but not rude. All the callers were on my side. When it was over, and off-air, the host gave me a big hug.

Keep your cool. Use every opportunity.

PUBLIC SERVICE ANNOUNCEMENTS

Do not forget to place your local events on the free and available community spaces for public service announcements (PSAs). Every newspaper, radio, and television station has opportunities for community bulletin boards. These opportunities for your message are tied to specific events—meetings, concerts, gatherings. Demonstrations ("We will be meeting on the lawn of the legislature to call for the removal of the current secretary of the environment...") are not likely to meet the non-confrontational nature of PSAS.

Although the standard PSA doesn't contain much of your message, the fact that your group's name is mentioned is a plus. If it is announced that "the Committee to Save Magic Creek is holding its monthly meeting" you are reminding people to save Magic Creek. I know of groups who have seized on the opportunity of major blizzards to invent meetings to cancel. With major weather events, cancellations are read out on the radio over and over again. "The meeting of the Friends of the Sacred Grove is cancelled due to the weather" is an announcement that gives your group profile—and may surprise members who did not know there was supposed to be a meeting!

Sometimes you can develop a thirty-second message for radio or television that will be accepted as in the public interest. These have to also be quite tame. A good PSA, however, can be played over and over as stations prefer to fill their required community-service time with messages that are clever and engaging. Often advertising agencies will donate their services for a good cause and will experiment with a catchy message. These thirty seconds of air time can win prizes for the ad agency, make television managers happy, and get your message on TV without paying commercial ad rates. Launching a clever, well-produced thirty-second PSA can also get you time on the evening news.

One of the cleverest ads of this type I ever worked on was to call for legislation to protect the habitat of endangered species. The concept of the ad was brilliant. It placed endangered species in urban settings, looking like homeless people. It pointed out that a cougar and a grizzly bear need homes. The catch line: "Give them a law with teeth."[11]

Delivering on the concept turned out to be a serious challenge. Libraries of endangered species video were searched for animals in attitudes and positions that would fit an urban setting. Finding none, new footage was taken in zoos. High-tech studio work plunked the cougar on an urban fire escape, and a grizzly bear near a sidewalk vent in downtown Toronto. The ad was high-quality and hugely watchable. Launched to television stations, the spot initially garnered both print-media and electronic-media coverage and then started running for free.

THE BRAVE NEW WORLD OF COMMUNICATIONS: INTERNET MEDIA, BLOGGING, AND WEB PAGES

With the advent of the World Wide Web there is a whole new world of communications tactics. While most of the benefit of the Internet to non-governmental organizations (NGOs) has been through information sharing and strategies between groups and individuals,[12] the Web also offers nearly free opportunities to get the word out. Even small citizens' groups put up their own home pages to make information about their concerns accessible. Getting their Web address published on everything from fridge magnets to small newspaper ads can direct interested people to the detailed information that used to cost far more as printed literature.

There are other ways to get the word out. Vermont governor Howard Dean will go down in history as the first U.S. presidential candidate to successfully use the Internet to build his campaign base. In the race to become the Democratic Party nominee in 2004, he used Internet sites that allowed people to meet up, and posted times and places of meetings, directed people to his home page and campaign promises.

Dean's Meetup.com worked through zip codes, linking people in the same community and allowing them to attend local meetings. During the Democratic nomination race, there were more than six hundred Dean Meetup meetings across the U.S. every month. When Vice-President Dick Cheney held a two-thousand-dollar-a-plate fundraising dinner, the Dean Web site posted a picture of the candidate eating a three-dollar turkey sandwich and asked for donations. The Web-site's turkey-sandwich appeal raised five hundred thousand dollars in three days.

Blogging messages (posting your own Web logs), has another type of audience. The potential for cyber-campaigning is just beginning to be harnessed.

As well, there is a whole new branch of the media, posting Internet journals. The famous *Drudge Report* in the U.S. has run with stories more conventional journalists would not have found to pass the sniff test. For the green movement, the U.S. Internet "zine" *Grist* provides a summary of other news items as well as original articles. In Canada, a number of very good sources of information for people concerned with social change and the environment are published on-line. Feminist and media commentator Judy Rebick came up with Rabble.com while Ish Theilhammer has a longer history as founder of Straightgoods.com.

These news sources fall into the category of "indie media." They are not a complete fit with self-posted Web items, but are more likely to take your group's news releases and articles and post them without re-writes.

In an in-between zone lie listservs of all shapes and sizes. In some ways they are primarily internal communications tools, but can be ways to reach to new segments of the public. If you are campaigning on a public health issue, maybe a listserv set up by groups opposing new trade agreements paving the way to privatization will allow your message to be posted to their list. Environmental groups have many sub-affiliations. If you are working primarily on a fossil fuel issue with a group of supporters motivated by concerns about climate change, you can reach a different base by posting a message connecting the threat to wilderness with fossil fuel developments, and climate change impacts to a list serving wilderness activists.

There is no point in setting down here what is possible on the Internet as it will be out of date by the time the book goes to print. It will not be long before environmental groups are able to film their own newscasts and stream them to the Web, highlighting the important events overlooked by the mainstream, advertising-dollar-driven television network news. What is timeless advice is this: constantly innovate and grab whatever techniques are available at a low price to reach the maximum number of people.

No matter how seductive the new technology, no matter how many bells and whistles you add to your Web site, remember that nothing motivates people to become involved like personal, not virtual, contact. The plodding and timeworn techniques of local organizing meetings will still be your mainstay.

PAID ADVERTISING

In the thirty years and the dozens of campaigns I have worked in the environmental movement, I have paid for advertising so rarely that each occasion sticks in my mind. Ads cost too much money for most of us. To make a serious impact on policy questions, a full-page ad is ideal, but a full-page ad in the national Canadian paper, the *Globe and Mail* is fifty-five thousand dollars (non-profit rate.) A full-page ad in the *New York Times* is similarly priced for non-government groups, but you are not guaranteed the day on which it will be placed. Can it possibly be worth it?

Generally not, but used in critical moments, full-page ads ·can be worth the expense.

To have such a huge financial commitment make sense, you need to choose the right moment with a well-crafted message. The movement to stop atmospheric nuclear weapons testing broke through a wall of denial in the United States in the early 1960s with a full-page ad in the *New York Times*. I can still see it in my mind's eye (and I was six!). Doyle, Dane and Burnbach, a top Madison Avenue ad agency, donated their creative talent. The ad was minimalist: four-fifths of the page was a picture; words only filled the bottom fifth. The long, vertical image was of everyone's favourite baby doctor, Benjamin Spock. He was wearing his standard (in those days) three-piece suit, with watch fob. His hands rested on the shoulders of a small girl and he was looking down at her, concern etched into his face. The headline was simple: "Dr. Spock is worried."

The text went on to describe the threat of radioactive fall-out to children's health. Bear in mind, this was the first political step Spock had ever taken. The impact was huge.

Timing can be everything. At the height of the Kyoto ratification debate in Canada, in the fall of 2002 as the vote approached, the industry "coalition"[13] spent millions of dollars in advertising in a last-ditch effort to erode public support. There were saturation-level television advertisements and regular full-page newspaper ads. It felt overwhelming. I had no money for anything at that point in my discretionary Sierra Club of Canada funds (generally that is the case!) for a full-page ad, but I felt that we needed something to fight back. We started calling and writing to as many well-known, and not so well-known Canadians, asking them to sign on to a statement in favour of Kyoto. By category we approached writers (Farley Mowat. Margaret Atwood, Michael Ondaatje), musicians (Barenaked Ladies, Tragically Hip, Bruce Cockburn), artists (Robert Bateman), religious leaders (Canadian Conference of Catholic Bishops, Rabbi Bulka), actors (R.H. Thomson, Sarah Polley, John Neville), comedians (Greg Malone, Cathy Jones), Olympic athletes, community volunteers whose work had been recognized by the Order of Canada, business leaders (CEO of Tembec, Frank Detorri, CEO of Husky Injection Molding, Robert Schad, and former CEO of McMillan Bloedel, Adam Zimmerman), and professional athletes (former CFL player, Gabriel Gregoire). All of the above and about one hundred others readily agreed. What is more, most agreed to donate five hundred to one thousand dollars towards the cost of running the ad.

We planned a press conference in Toronto that happened to coincide with the Gemini Awards for performing artists so more could be in Toronto. The press conference was on a Tuesday; the ad would be full page in the *Globe and Mail* on Thursday. With any luck we would get electronic coverage of the "prominent Canadians speak out for Kyoto" press conference on Tuesday, print coverage of it on Wednesday, the ad would hit Thursday and we would get stories about the ad on Friday. In fact, we got all of that coverage and more. Key *Globe and Mail* commentators, the ever-balanced and reasonable Hugh Winsor and anti-Kyoto hysteric Rex Murphy, both wrote columns respectively commenting and attacking our ad. So I got another letter-to-the-editor opportunity to the paper to reply to Murphy's thesaurus-challenging diatribe. The national CBC Radio morning program had a panel discussion of the rival pro- and anti-Kyoto advertising campaigns, and our one-time-only ad in the *Globe* was treated as equivalent to the non-stop corporate propaganda. The reason we got so much coverage was that the ad concept got a last-minute dose of Madison Avenue pizzazz.

One of the signatories, Michael de Pencier of Key Publishing, volunteered that he had some creative geniuses in marketing who he would ask to make the ad stand out. Grant Gordon went to work. I made it hard for him by saying the text the signatories had agreed to was one arrived at through real negotiation and a lot of back-and-forth discussion. I refused to have the text, which Gordon thought had too many words for an ad, be completely dropped. He rose to the challenge with a memorable, cheeky, and attention grabbing heading. The largest word on the page was the first: "QUICK" then "Name ten prominent Canadians who are against Kyoto. (You can't can you? No one can.)"

Then it picked up the text with the linking phrase, "On the other hand, naming ten prominent Canadians who support Kyoto is a walk in the park. There are more than a hundred listed below who agree that…"

The ad worked. It had chutzpah. It had impact. But the single largest factor justifying the decision to place resources in paid advertising was timing. The time was right. Ironically, thanks to the deluge of industry advertising, a moment had been created when our ad would be noticed.

THE BEST PAID AD IS ONE YOU DO NOT USE

From time to time you can make an ad work for you without actually using it. A brutally effective ad that a corporation or politician does *not* want to see in the newspaper can actually win the whole campaign. Environmental lawyer Robert Kennedy Jr. once developed a series of newspaper ads opposing the City of New York's decision to cancel spending on sewage control. The ads were graphic in communicating the message that sewage would be getting into drinking-water sources if the mayor's decision was not reversed. One of the series showed male genitalia with hot and cold water taps in strategic locations.

Before buying space in the *New York Times*, Kennedy took the ads to a meeting with the mayor. The mayor changed his mind on the spot.

I have sat across a boardroom table from a Canadian forest industry CEO and showed a mock-up of a billboard aimed at U.S. newspapers buying their paper: a panoramic view of Canadian forest and the tag line: "Your morning paper could be printed on this. Tell the *Philadelphia Inquirer* you want to protect the oldest forest ecosystems on the planet." As a result of viewing the ad, negotiations for protection opened up. To use advertisements as leverage to change decisions you must ensure that the threat is credible. The ads should be ready to go. The organization should have the capacity to run such a campaign. You do not need to have purchased the ad space, but you need to at least sound ready to do so.

The purpose of the ad is to impact a decision-maker. If you can cut out the middleman by taking the ad to its target, so much the better.

LESSONS LEARNED:

1) Look for your free opportunities to reach your community.
2) Use your head.
3) Reach the public anyway you can.

4) To get good media coverage, be a media junkie.

5) Get those letters to the editor published! It is the most-read section of your newspaper.

6) Tell all your friends and supporters when you are on open-line radio.

7) Don't tell your mother!

8) Buy advertising only when the time is right. Make sure your ad will be noticed.

9) Remember to send out your public service announcements regularly. They are free.

10) Always ask for a deal. Always ask for a discount. You may get lucky.

Chapter 7

PUBLIC MOBILIZATION

EVERY STEP YOU TAKE IN CAMPAIGNING should be aimed at increasing your visibility and credibility to the larger amorphous "public." Your message is clear and well-buttressed by facts. Your message has reached the news media and been relayed to thousands or millions through newspaper and television.

How do you translate that level of coverage to tangible evidence of public support?

The tools of public mobilization move through an escalating hierarchy of steps requiring ever-greater levels of commitment. You want to provide easy steps for the uninitiated, moving to actions that require deeper involvement. Step by step, lead people from petitions to postcards to letters to events, and to demonstrations.

Do you remember the ParticipAction campaign? Canadians were labelled "couch potatoes." We were told that a sixty-year-old Swede was in better shape than a thirty-year-old Canadian. The first advertisements did not suggest we get into shape for a ten-kilometre run. The first ad simply suggested, "Walk a block a day." Then our level of fitness expectations began to shift. We started joining health clubs and entering marathons. Think about mobilizing the public to political action the same way we were mobilized to get up off the couch. The action equivalent of walking a block a day is signing a petition. The Iron Man competition is like a fourteen-year battle to save a precious piece of wilderness. Never ask people to take the next step until they are ready.

PETITIONS ARE EFFECTIVE ORGANIZING TOOLS

Petitions are an old and accepted way of reaching government. A petition to the king has been a means of lobbying for centuries. The Declaration of Independence was one of the world's most elegant and effective petitions. It was short, to the point, and evocative. It did not succeed in reaching King George to grant independence to the colonies, but it did lay the intellectual groundwork for a revolution.

A petition campaign is a great first step for any neophyte group. Its virtues are many. Preparing the petition requires boiling your concerns down to their essentials. Distributing petitions enlists as many volunteers as you can recruit. The delivery of petitions to a decision-maker is a newsworthy event. And, ultimately, your petitions influence policy.

The first element of a petition is to choose the appropriate decision-maker. Are you hoping to reach a decision-maker at the national or local level? If your petition is to the House of Commons, you need to use the traditional language for submission to the House.[14] Your preamble series of "whereas" clauses should be no longer than one-third to half the page. Each clause should speak to a different element of your concerns: economic, health-related, environmental damage, etc. Each line is like a brick, laying the foundation for your request.

The key action you are demanding of government is in your last line, "Therefore, we the undersigned, request that the Minister of Everything immediately prohibit the...."

The rest of the page is lined with headings for signature, printed name and address. The very bottom of the petition should include the name of the group circulating the petition, its mailing address, Web site, and/or phone number.

Remember that every movement benefits from early successes. Run your petition campaign with clear goals. Depending on the size of the group and extent of the population concerned, choose an ambitious, but achievable, target number of signatures by a specific date. Do not leave your petition campaign open-ended or petitions will gather dust. Five thousand names on petitions within three months is reasonable; a million names over the next four years is not.

Gathering names on petitions presents a myriad of possibilities for any group. You can rely on members asking friends and workplace colleagues. You can establish information pickets by using clipboards and stationing yourselves near the entrance to a location with some symbolic connection to the campaign. You can set up a table in a farmers' market or shopping mall.

BEING MALLED

The mall experience can be discouraging. It is going into the ethical wilderness; a dead zone of florescent lighting and consumerism. To attract people to your table to talk about the issues, you need to be non-threatening and very friendly. A permanent smile must be fixed to your face. Look up expectantly and ask pleasantly, "Can you take a minute to help us save Emerald Woods?" As people pass you by as though you have something contagious, resist any temptation to retort. Keep on smiling, "Maybe next time. Have a nice day."

Your presence in a public place is helpful on many levels. You may find new volunteers. People who have read about your group's efforts receive a subtle reinforcement that the group is a legitimate effort of local residents. Ideally, your volunteers staffing the table are dressed conventionally. Mall work is grim. Appealing to the average shopper you need to look like an average shopper. Your mall table is not a place to send your blue-haired, multi-tattooed, and pierced volunteers.

One of the most successful petition campaigns in recent years was conducted by a handful of our local volunteers in Sydney, Nova Scotia, when the government announced there would be a thirty-day period to gauge public reaction to a proposed "clean up" of the Sydney Tar Ponds, involving incineration of some PCB-contaminated sludge and the burial in concrete of over six hundred thousand tonnes of toxic waste. It took a week to agree on the petition language, so the time to collect names on the petitions shrank to twenty days. Yet, amazingly in a relatively small community they collected over four thousand signatures before the deadline. When I asked them how they had done it, Debbie Ouellette said most of the credit had to go to her puppy. She couldn't leave the two-month-old puppy at home, so Ouellette brought her along to the mall and farmers' market. The puppy was an irresistible attraction. Once over at the table, people realized what the petition was about and signed eagerly. Get a puppy! In malls that do not allow pets, bring a baby; adorable and gurgling is best.

Other good public locations are farmers' markets, where people may be more friendly and relaxed. Another possibility is to ask sympathetic merchants if you can set up at the entrance to their store. Mountain Equipment Co-Op in Canada is very helpful in letting environmental groups have a good indoor spot for petitioning. You can also do the "table-less" petition effort. Being stationed in busy pedestrian areas with a clipboard and a smile can also work.

Petition campaigns can influence governments in all sorts of ways. I recall during the campaign against the Multilateral Agreement on Investment (MAI) telling a Member of Parliament that the issue was crucial and of real concern to Canadians. He simply did not believe me, until he returned from a parliamentary trip that took him through Newfoundland. In a gas station in Corner Brook, a petition against the MAI was filling up. He was convinced.

When you reach your goal of X names by X date, arrange a public presentation of the petitions. It is always a good idea to photocopy all the petitions to have a record of your supporters. You can phone people who signed a petition to let them know about any local events you are planning. Give the originals to the key decision-maker or her representative. If a government representative will not attend your event to receive the petitions, ask a member of the Opposition. Manage to display the petitions in such a way that the thousands of names have maximum impact.

Afterwards, give yourselves a reward. Take a breather from meetings and have a purely social event to celebrate.

LETTER-WRITING CAMPAIGNS

The next step up from petitions is the letter, originally composed to the decision-maker. Form texts are not nearly as effective.

Postcard campaigns are popular and fall in-between petitions and letters in terms of impact. Many groups have adopted postcards for the dual purpose of influencing politicians and collecting names for future fundraising. (When an organization asks for you to send a postcard of concern to the organization for them to forward to the decision-maker, you are giving them your name for later mailings.) Postcards with form messages are rarely individually answered by politicians and not given much more weight than petitions.

Because so few people take the time to write a letter on an issue that concerns them, politicians count each letter as representative of the views of far more citizens. A letter to a federal politician is seen as representing thousands. Provincial and local representatives also recognize the letter of one person as being representative of many more.

Letters are a tried-and-true way of reaching elected officials. Sierra Club founder John Muir led a legendary (and sadly unsuccessful) fight to stop the construction of the Hetch Hetchy Dam in the early part of the twentieth century. Muir used all the same elements that I am describing here. He used the media, with major articles in the most popular magazine of the era, *Colliers*. Muir was one of the most popular authors of the period and his articles were accompanied with engraved illustrations of the magnificent waterfalls of the Hetch Hetchy. Muir called for public support and the response was overwhelming. The public uproar was nationwide. One congressman reported that he had received five thousand letters opposing the construction of the dam. Imagine. Over five thousand handwritten letters in the days before computers, fax machines, e-mails, or even Xerox.

One thing has not changed in the last century, despite all the technological change. Politicians still give credence to a letter. A handwritten letter is virtually the most effective letter you can send. A typed (now "word processed") letter is fine, but an e-mail is virtually useless. Few politicians have adapted to consider an e-mail as nearly as important as a paper letter. I have talked to staff in offices of members of Parliament who simply hit the delete button for incoming e-mails, especially if the office is being inundated by electronic form letters.

Who knows how long this anachronistic state of affairs will continue, but at this writing, *to have an impact in Canada, use snail mail*: unless the issue is urgent and requires sending a fax (with the original arriving by post later), use the postal system. As a small but added bonus, no stamps are required for letters to Canadian MPs.

In the United States, for letters destined for Washington, D.C. to congressmen and senators, use the telephone, fax, and e-mail. Unfortunately, since September 11 and the various anthrax scares, getting a letter to a senator's office now takes three weeks longer than it used to. As well, the mail arrives somewhat damaged. I've heard it described as "parchment."

Letters have an impact in the system. Each letter is answered, or should be! As the numbers of letters pile up on a particular issue, the "system" begins to notice. First, the poor, overworked civil servant who has to prepare responses on your issue begins to notice the workload increase. The concern starts being registered up the food chain, to directors, then Assistant Deputy Ministers and finally to the Minister's office. The *vox populi* does get noticed. When I worked in the Minister of the Environment's office, the number of letters calling for the protection of South Moresby weighed in to critical decisions. I remember listening to my boss, Tom McMillan, then Minister of the Environment, as he spoke by phone with his boss, Prime Minister Mulroney: "We are getting more letters on saving South Moresby than any other issue. Even more letters than on acid rain." Protecting South Moresby had a lot to do with having enough letters from Canadians from coast to coast.

HOW DO YOU MOBILIZE PEOPLE TO WRITE LETTERS?

A letter-writing campaign is an excellent organizing tool. To generate thousands of letters, you need to give concerned people the tools to write an effective letter. Key elements of your tool kit are:

- A crisp, clear fact sheet—set out the key facts of the proposal you oppose, the alternatives, the key ecological features, economic arguments, with citations of authoritative bodies and experts whose quotes may be used;
- A sample letter (with explicit instructions *not* to just copy it!). Encourage people to keep letters relatively short and to the point;
- Be clear that the letters be original and are best if they do not appear connected to any particular environmental group effort;
- Up-to-date names and addresses for key decision-makers.

The tool kit for a letter writing campaign should be available on your Web site and in a paper version.

Letter writing should happen all the time, but a letter-writing campaign should have a beginning and an end to focus energy. Set a goal (e.g., tell your supporters you need to have five hundred letters into the office of the secretary of the interior by Christmas). To get the ball rolling, hold letter-writing bees. Invite people to your house for potluck and then sit down and crank out the letters. Provide envelopes, paper (different types), and pens and take care of getting the letters mailed. You can also set up letter-writing bees at community events, fairs, and at after-worship coffee hours.

Remember the advice about giving talented volunteers tasks they will enjoy. That volunteer I mentioned in the last chapter—ghost-writing letters to the editor—can also produce letters for other people to sign.

To have an impact, your letter need not be a treatise. It need not reflect expert views. All the letter needs to convey is that a) issue X matters to you; and b) you want to know where the decision-maker stands on the issue.

Wherever possible, ask your supporters to send you copies of any answers received. This effort keeps them feeling connected with your group and the issue. Forwarding a letter received from the Minister of Fisheries to the organizer, even if everyone has received identical replies from the minister, will increase the level of commitment of that individual to the larger group. The reply is itself an accomplishment, though modest. The letter-writer is subliminally empowered by their name and address appearing in close proximity to the elected official. It is very subtle, but even the most sophisticated citizen experiences a sense of power in circulating the prime minister's or president's reply.

Writing original letters takes time. Maximize your efforts by sending the letter to the prime minister or premier with a copy to other relevant cabinet ministers. The letter will register throughout the system.

PUBLIC EVENTS

When you feel you have a critical mass of committed people, hold a public event. Public events are media events, public outreach to gain more supporters, and can also be fundraisers.

Public events let you be proactive. You can choose the date, the location, and organize a program of your choosing.

THE DATE: Choose the date that gives plenty of organizing lead time. Before you nail yourself down to a particular date, make a concerted effort to find out what else is going on in your community that night. Do not hold your event the same night as the free fireworks and open concert in the town centre. Do your best to avoid major sporting events. I do not have a clue about sports, but know that if your event is during the Grey Cup or World Series, you will make your job running a successful event much harder.

THE LOCATION: Unlike demonstrations, usually held in some location reflective of opposition (i.e., in front of the legislature, in front of corporate headquarters, etc), the public event is on your turf. Choose a well-known, easily found location. Avoid spending money on your venue. Library theatres, civic facilities, a school auditorium, even church halls, can accommodate a speaker and slide show, a public panel with a vigorous question-and-answer session, a musical evening with information interspersed.

THE PROGRAM: Be creative. You can offer a well-known speaker who draws a crowd. You can put on a slide show introducing people to the beauty of the place you want to save. You can offer a satirical look at the issue through theatre. Or, failing to get a government panel hearing, you can organize your event as a "Peoples' Inquiry." The sky's the limit. The only rule is not to plan an event that will bore your audience.

GETTING THE WORD OUT

Advertising your event is a form of publicity for the cause. Using public service announcements you can get your issue mentioned on community calendars on radio, television, and newspapers. Ensure you notify all members of your group and anyone who has expressed an interest. In the cyber-age, people tend to rely on an e-mail announcement to inform the committed supporters. An e-mail announcement is essential, but it is not enough. To get people to turn out for an event, you need a much more personal approach. A phone tree is still, despite the advent of electronic communication, a very valuable tool. People need to hear another human voice. That voice must express need: "We really need you to attend."

It is a common failing in organizers to assume that if people know about an event and the event features a major celebrity, a large turn out is assured. One of my mother's early experiences was in attending a public lecture by one of her heroes, Eleanor Roosevelt. The First Lady had been invited to Hartford by a group to speak in a major local hall. Six people showed up. The organizers were devastated and embarrassed. Their mistake was simple. They had not worked hard in advance to mobilize a crowd.

Tom d'Aquino, spokesperson for corporate Canada, once referred pejoratively to Maude Barlow, volunteer chairperson for the Council of Canadians, as using "rent-a-crowd." There is no such thing. Getting out a crowd requires two things: a large group of people who support your cause; and a lot of hard work, phoning, cajoling, and begging people to turn out.

To get commitments to attend meetings, delegate jobs to lots of people. Ask someone to bring name tags, someone else to set up the coffee. Make sure you have a core of committed attendees so your event will have a respectable turn out. Hope for more to show up off the street, but do not count on a strong turn out from unidentifiable supporters.

Make one last round of calls to remind reporters about the event. For those who indicate they will not be able to attend, try to create an alternative opportunity. Offer your speaker for an earlier interview. Suggest that the key points can be shared in advance. Explore options to get your event in the media.

THE FAIR

Holding your own fair is lots of work offset by lots of fun. I have organized them in rural areas in a big community hall, or taken over Sparks Street Mall in downtown Ottawa. They work everywhere. Your key ingredients are tables set up for local eco-vendors and environmental groups—flea market-style. Have people reserve a table and pay a nominal amount to your group for participating. Tables of baked goods, organic veggies, jams and jellies can be judged just like in the old agricultural fairs. Offer a Blue Ribbon. Sell the goodies. Have sidewalk chalk for kids to decorate the town. (You may need to have a crew to mop up later!) Invite buskers, clowns, and local bands. All the same rules for planning and getting out the crowd still apply!

THE DEMONSTRATION

This is your ten-kilometre run. This is your evidence that people are truly committed and are prepared to step outside their personal comfort zone and be seen in a march or rally, holding a picket sign, chanting chants, and expressing themselves on the street. (As an aside, we really need better chants. We used to have "Two, four, six, eight! Stop the war, Negotiate," and "Ho, ho, Ho Chi Minh! The NLF (National Liberation Front) is going to win." Now we seem to be stuck with "Hey, hey! Ho, Ho! Whatever it is has got to go." All we are saying is give chants a chance.)

My cousin Lois from Charleston, South Carolina, was clearly baffled by my mother's activism. She knew my mother was one of those people she sometimes saw on the news, marching and protesting. She asked, "but how do y'all know when to do it?" It was clearly a vast mystery to her how thousands of people can all show up at the same time.

When one million people congregate in a major city and all express a shared concern it is an overwhelming experience. It was thrilling to march with one million people in New York City in the 1982 March for Peace in conjunction with the UN General Assembly Special Session on Disarmament. We filled whole blocks. We were in a gridlock of humanity. We knew that just up ahead in Central Park was a free concert and rally with Paul Simon and other major stars. As it turned out we never could get into the packed park. And it did not matter. Decades before, I had walked those same streets as the slow steady chant of "Peace now" reverberated from the skyscrapers. The end point of the march was the United Nations where Dr. Martin Luther King was speaking to our assembled masses in an outdoor rally. I will never forget, at age ten, the wonder of hearing his voice over a transistor radio, knowing that he was just out of sight, a few blocks ahead, with the street blocked and progress impossible. It did not matter then either that the success of the march meant I could not reach the speakers. It is always an extraordinary thing to be part of a loving mass of humanity. Being part of an enormous gathering of people with a shared cause is cathartic. It provokes euphoric smiles and wonderful memories. A well-run, peaceful, large gathering also influences politicians.

HOW DO YOU GET PEOPLE INTO THE STREETS? WHEN IS IT TIMELY?

Mass mobilization of people in the streets is a culturally constrained phenomenon. It is easier to get huge marches in India than in France. It is easier to get large crowds in France than in the United States. It is easier to get large crowds in the United States than in Canada.

If a demonstration needs several thousand people to be a success, never proceed if you can only identify fifteen who will be there for sure. Politicians and the media may gauge the strength of your public support by the number of people you can mobilize. It is the opposite of the old slogan, "What if they gave a war and nobody came?" You do not want to find out what happens if there is a demonstration and nobody comes.

A demonstration or rally makes sense when a situation is urgent, a government is about to make a bad decision, or a company's performance needs to have a light of public awareness directed on its activities.

When you hold a march, if at all possible, find a few bagpipers to head the line of march. The average person who feels hostile to a passing group of protesters will turn and smile at the rousing skirl of the pipes. (This is, of course, also a culturally specific suggestion. Works best in Canada!)

A rally makes sense with an outdoor concert or celebratory event. Earth Day, April 22 is a good choice. Decades are better than off-years: Earth Day 1990 was inevitably a bigger event than Earth Day 1991.

A big demonstration requires a long lead time and lots of resources. You need to mobilize bus loads of people from beyond your community. Logistics must be painstakingly considered. Food, accomodation, appropriate permits, sound systems, parade marshals with proper training must all be attended to.

Increasingly, large demonstrations at the focal points of institutions viewed as inherently evil—the World Trade Organization, the World Bank Board of Governors, the World Economic Summit—are drawing large crowds. For the first time in my life, tear gas is being used, not rarely, but routinely. From Seattle to Genoa to Quebec City, protests have been met with violence, while a only small proportion of the protesters planned to do violence, at least to property. The police reaction is often an overreaction. There was no need in Quebec City to create a weather system of tear gas. The "threat" from protesters was one that could have been handled less disruptively with sensible arrests.[15] These are disturbing trends. The only type of protest that is effective is peaceful protest.[16]

A smaller demonstration can be effective so long as the organizers take pains to ensure public, media, and government expectations are not raised to believe that thousands of people are expected. Good strategies for demonstrations that work with smaller numbers include silent vigils, candlelight observances, street theatre (such in mass "die-ins"),[17] information pickets, and any event involving children asking politicians to take action. Invite the Raging Grannies ("Only in Canada, you say? Pity.")

THE ONE-PERSON PROTEST

The ultimate small demonstration is the hunger strike. It is not a common form of protest in North America, with the exception of prisoners. It is difficult and can present serious health risks. Nevertheless, it can create significant media attention to your issue. It can engage government in a different way. The urgency of the situation grows with the length of the hunger strike as concerns about health begin to mount.

I went on a hunger strike once. Although I began imagining that my fast might last a week, it lasted seventeen days. I doubt I would do it again, but only because I promised so many friends I wouldn't. It was actually a very positive experience.

I felt pushed to take drastic action over the situation of residents living near the Sydney Tar Ponds—Canada's largest toxic waste site, located virtually in the middle of town and surrounded by homes, schools, day care centres, and playgrounds. A new set of soil samples for heavy metals and toxic substances had found sky-high levels. I knew the predictable government response would be a health-risk assessment. I have become convinced that these computer-generated modelling efforts are designed to minimize risk and provide cover for hazardous situations. It seemed entirely likely that (as did happen), people would be left to manage with contamination all around them. I thought sitting in front of Parliament Hill and demanding that the Minister of Health act to move families away from areas of extensive toxic contamination might be the only way to get quick action.

The act of sitting in front of Parliament on a hunger strike may have been one of the most effective things I've ever done. It certainly built relationships in new ways. It was before the post–September 11 additional security around the House of Commons. I was able to be on the sidewalk opposite the door to the House, and every MP and cabinet minister knew I was there. Most came and spoke with me. Members of Parliament who would never have been sympathetic to most environmental issues, agreed with me about the plight of residents in Sydney. Many people prayed for me. People of all parties were concerned and understood that a hunger strike meant that I was not just some lobbyist working in the environmental movement. My hunger strike was the first time some MPs realized my work was an outgrowth of personal commitment.

I found the time enlightening. My time for prayer and thoughtfulness increased. My mental and intellectual energy was heightened and stimulated. Sadly, Health Minister Alan Rock's promise to move residents, which ended my hunger strike, was never honoured. Instead, the government conducted the anticipated health-risk assessment that denied any health risk. Most of the residents about whom I was most alarmed still live with contaminated soil. Current provincial government plans will leave them with contamination in backyards and homes, even after the "cleanup" is complete. If I ever go on another hunger strike, it will be for the same issue and for the same people.

My hunger strike was entirely peaceful. It was entirely legal (I even had a permit to sit on Parliament Hill). In certain circumstances (and only on the advice of your doctor) a hunger strike is worth considering.

THE CARAVAN

Another great tool for mobilizing people, literally, is the caravan—a movable demonstration from town to town. In 1993, Sierra Club of Canada organized a cross-country rail caravan to raise support for Clayoquot Sound. We started at Mile Zero in St. John's, Newfoundland (by bus) hooking up with Via Rail where it begins in Halifax, across Canada to Vancouver, and then by bus to Clayoquot Sound. One of our favourite wags titled the Clayoquot Express as travelling "from the ocean without fish to the forest without trees." We made stops in fourteen towns for whistle-stop rallies as local people came out to show their support. We made four overnight stops, disembarking, and being billeted to allow for concerts and fundraisers in Halifax, Ottawa, Toronto, and Vancouver. We had on-board child care, on-board composting, organic food for snacks, our own sound system for workshops and lectures as we rolled through the Canadian landscape, and a brilliant folksinger and consummate entertainer, Holly Arntzen. We were an instant rally as we poured out of the train—whether at midday at Union Station in Toronto or at three in the morning in Saskatoon. The Clayoquot Express had a romance and magic to it that goes with train travel. More than 150 people took part, travelling some or all of the way. A few had only been planning on attending a railway station rally, but, swept up in the excitement, bought a ticket on the spot and jumped aboard without so much as a toothbrush.

It was a huge amount of work, but we reached people in a very different way. For those who travelled together, it was literally a life-altering experience. For those who attended the rallies or read local coverage, it increased awareness of the Clayoquot issue.

Youth activists have had major impacts with bicycle caravans. Through the spring and summer of 2002, the Climate Change Caravan rolled across Canada, from British Columbia to Newfoundland. They stopped in many communities, offered talks to schools, held public meetings, gave press conferences, and held "critical mass" rallies.[18] They travelled with patches of colourful fabric for a climate change flag. People they met along the way added their own climate-change message to the fabric. Over fifty young people (and some not so young!) joined in. The caravan was accompanied by a side vehicle, an old school bus lugging the gear and kitchen, and fuelled by a dual diesel and vegetable oil engine. Having adapted the vehicle to allow a switch over from the diesel tank to the used vegetable oil tank, they spent a lot of time educating mechanics about climate change while repairs were made to a chronically broken-down engine. It definitely attracted local media interest when it became known that the bus was fuelled with used vegetable oil picked up for free at the local Golden Arches. The caravaners reported they always knew when the driver had switched tanks because they could smell french fries.

CONCLUSION

Mobilizing people to take action is essential. Even people who agree with you may see themselves as a bystander to the passing parade. They wish to cheer you from the sidelines. To win on our issues, we have to move bystanders to participants. Make the transition from bystander to participant as non-threatening as possible. Start with the easy steps. Support, encourage, and thank your supporters and volunteers at every step along the way. When the parade is full and the sidewalk is empty, we have won.

Actually, the minority wins any campaign (or revolution). A large mass of any nation or community will stay apathetic. They do not even go out to watch the parade. That's okay. We only need to bring a critical mass of about 15 percent of the public into active support for our causes to triumph. This is good news.

Those who take action have a disproportionate impact. The power of one is to move many.

LESSONS LEARNED:

1) Mobilizing the public is key.
2) Start with the easy steps.
3) Asking someone to sign a petition is easier than asking them to chain themselves to the premier.
4) Write letters by hand.
5) Have fun while generating public awareness and increased engagement.
6) There is no "rent-a-crowd."
7) Invite a bagpiper.
8) Be creative.
9) Come up with a few singable songs and chantable chants!
10) Thank everyone who helps. (I know. You've seen this lesson before. But it's not for nothing we were taught that "please" and "thank you" are the magic words.)

Chapter 8
LOBBYING

THE WORD "LOBBYING" CARRIES a lot of baggage. It evokes images of the big-bellied, cigar-smoking, three-martini lunch characters of old political dramas. The word comes from the historical use of the government lobby. Those hoping to bend the ear of members of the British Parliament would hang out in the lobby area just off the legislative chamber. There was another famous lobby in a Washington hotel, where politicians would be buttonholed. Over a century ago, the noun "lobby" became a verb meaning bending the ears of politicians.

One of the fastest growth areas in political capitals, with new firms popping up like dandelions in summer, is "government-relations consulting." Large amounts of money are spent by those with deep pockets to get access to decision-makers.

Another piece of baggage is the fact that the "L" word is a "no-no" for the taxman in dealing with charitable dollars. In the United States, groups must be very careful in segregating their "501 (c) (3) and 501 (c) (4)" money. The U.S. Internal Revenue Code uses these sections to define what a charitable organization is allowed to do. (C) (3) money is charitable and cannot be used for advocacy and lobbying. In Canada, the rule is that charities cannot spend more than 10 percent of their resources on attempts to impact government decision-making. In recent years, the rulings on this question have become increasingly restrictive, leading to complaints from philanthropic associations that the rules allow the feeding of the poor, but not finding ways to alleviate poverty.

Public-interest groups face a double-barreled problem. We do not have money for the "guns for hire." And we (if the organization is a charity) are fearful of losing charitable status by going over a line—a line that keeps shifting.

Despite these challenges, reaching the individual decision-makers is not just a good idea, it is *essential*.

In a democracy, access to our elected officials is not a privilege; it is a right. It should not be dependent on hiring a paid lobbyist. You can be your own lobbyist. And the good news is, the average citizen, a dedicated person committed to an issue without any financial interest in the outcome, makes the best impression on a politician. Sure, politicians can be influenced by big business. Nevertheless, a politician's primary goal is to stay in power. Staying in power requires getting re-elected. Being on the side of the angels now and then generally helps gain votes.

The late Warner Troyer, arguably Canada's first environmental journalist, used to say, "The mistake that we make with politicians is that we tend to anthropomorphicize. We forget that politicians are single-celled organisms susceptible only to heat, pressure and pain."

While Troyer's remark always draws a laugh, it is oversimplified. Pressure is needed. "Holding their feet to the fire" is another frequently used metaphor. Beyond pain, I have found that politicians are also moved by love, by friendships, kindness, and a fair and generous gratitude when the politician does the right thing. Conversely, I have found that a surprising number of people in public life have very thin skins. A perceived slight can be remembered, and count against you, for a long time. This does not mean you should pull your punches when criticizing bad policies that threaten the environment, or good health care, or any other important cause, but it does mean you should take care to depersonalize your attack. Sticking to the high road, keeping your comments directed to the policy and not the person, will generally deliver better results than an *ad hominem* attack. (One small downside is that media coverage increases when you slip off the high road and end up in the gutter. Just remember, there are real and long-term costs for a cheap shot. Politicians are around for a long time. If you and your issue want help, do not burn your bridges.)

To reach politicians, you will follow a lot of the same precepts as you use in your group or to reach media. Influencing politicians is also about *building relationships*. Never burn a bridge. Be respectful. Be empathetic. Try to put yourselves in their shoes. Imagine the barriers to the decision you are seeking. Create the openings that make it easier for the right decision to emerge.

Once you have developed your case, gotten the word out and mobilized the public, decision-makers will be noticing you. Your credibility is building. The time is ripe for a direct contact with the decision-maker.

It is time to make that appointment!

HOW TO GET IN THE DOOR

You can get a meeting with anyone you need to meet. It is a matter of time and persistence. (Remember the Quebec-based comedy troupe that actually got a direct phone call through to Her Majesty the Queen by pretending to be Prime Minister Chrétien.)

Barriers to access increase with the degree of power of the decision-maker. The more important the decision-maker, the more likely she is to have a barrage of gatekeepers.

To reach your local municipal councilor, pick up the phone. It is relatively easy. I was amazed to be asked at an activist training workshop years back by a very experienced local activist if it was *ethical* to phone a councillor before a key vote. This question was from a woman who clearly had a lot of experience trying to get changes through her municipal council. I was astounded. Of course it is ethical. It is critical! The more local the decision-maker, the more they gauge the importance of an issue by their direct personal experience of voter concerns. Phone them at their office. Phone them at home. Stop them on the street.

Actually this advice applies to *all* politicians. If you are waiting at a bus stop and see the Minister of Whatever strolling back from lunch, grab him. Be polite. Express your concern on whatever issue is on the top of your mind at the moment, or just express general support for a strong environmental action plan. For some crazy reason, politicians take random meetings with average folks on the street very seriously. The exchange stays with them. It becomes a touchstone on reality that a real live voter approached them directly with a concern. The more powerful the person, the rarer the experience will be. Remember that Prime Minister Chrétien *invented* conversations with homeless people to give credence to his view of the world.

SEIZE THE MOMENT

Imagine that you are killing time in Washington, D.C. on a Sunday morning and see an opportunity to lobby the U.S. president. Ian, a friend from Greenpeace U.K., was in Washington to lobby for the U.S. to ratify the Treaty to Protect the Antarctic. With nothing do on a spring Sunday, he was wandering aimlessly, pondering going to a museum, when he saw President Bill Clinton and the first lady heading into a church.

He ducked into the same church and seeking a place in an empty pew, sat immediately behind them. Being British, he was stunned with what he described as the "barbaric" custom in North American churches of exchanging the Peace of the Lord, in which parishioners stand, shake hands, or hug the people near them.

So now he had exchanged the Peace of the Lord with the U.S. president, but no request for the Antarctic had passed his lips. One reason that he told me this story is that I played a role in it. I had been a friend of Bill Clinton when he was at Yale Law School. I was in high school and we were both volunteers working for George McGovern for president. I had visited President Clinton not long before Ian had stayed at my place in Ottawa. "So," he reported breathlessly, "I knew I would have thirty seconds *max* to reach Clinton as he went by me on the way out of church and I had to get his attention, so I said, 'I'm a friend of Elizabeth May and just saw your picture in her house in Ottawa and I am here in Washington to make sure the U.S. ratifies the Treaty to Protect the Antarctic and it is so important for you to make sure this happens…'" Clinton stopped and spoke with him for a few minutes. The Antarctic treaty was ratified two weeks later.

Coincidence? Angels working overtime? Pure luck? We'll never know. But it does go to show that when you see an opportunity to make a difference, do not hold back.

You never know where a chance encounter can take you.

To arrange a planned meeting, it should not be difficult to reach your own member of the provincial, state, or federal legislature. The politician who travels during the week to Washington or Ottawa, will have a local constituency office. You should be able to get an appointment through the local office.

If you are trying to meet with someone at the cabinet level, getting a meeting does become more challenging. The first step is to write a letter requesting a meeting. Your letter of request should be very clear and should identify the issue you wish to discuss. Be sure to include a phone number for any calls from the scheduling assistant to the politician.

As soon as the letter is sent, start making your follow-up calls. Always ask for and make a note of the name of every person with whom you speak. Be polite, but persistent. Support staff in every office is virtually universally ignored. The voice that answers your call is not that of a machine. There is a real live person in the office you want to reach, so make a point of remembering names. You will stand out from the vast majority of callers if you make a personal connection. Be grateful. Be friendly. Do not take out your frustration with the non-responsiveness of the "system" on support staff.

Sometimes a scheduling assistant is able to press for you to get your appointment. With a last-minute meeting cancellation, an assistant can suggest now would be a good time to see that group from Save the Marsh.

You can also drop by and get to know the staff in offices around your legislature. The South Moresby crew used the charm and good looks of their two key organizers to schmooze, flatter, and chat up the staff in the office of the Environment Minister. Access definitely improved!

In the 1970s, I had a fabulous telephone relationship with the secretary to the premier of Nova Scotia. I had asked for her name when I first started calling to ask when cabinet might be considering allowing aerial insecticide spraying of Cape Breton's forests. Her initial approach was cool and professional. I always thanked her for her help. After a few months, she began giving me lots of encouragement. Her attitude was a window to what was going on in the premier's office. I will never forget the excitement of her voice telling me, "Keep it up! So far we have over three thousand letters against spraying and only sixteen in favour!"

PREPARING FOR YOUR MEETING

Once you have your meeting, you need to prepare. Who from your group will attend? How many people should attend? How will you handle the meeting? These are important questions. You do not want to go into a meeting with a hothead likely to lose his temper. You need to make a good impression. The minimum goal of your first meeting is to get a second meeting.

You do not want to bring more than three to four people to the meeting, but you should not go alone. Often, a large number of people may want to attend. The reason you should resist allowing more than three to four, or ideally two to three, is that a large number from your group will result in a less useful meeting. Your meeting will be more productive if it takes place in the minister's personal office. Ideally, you would like your discussion to be as candid as possible. If you insist on bringing eight people, the meeting will move to a departmental boardroom. The minister will not attend with one staff person, but is likely to fill in government ranks to equal the number of people you have brought. Suddenly, many opportunities for good communication have been removed and your meeting has slid away from dialogue and moved toward confrontation.

Be disciplined. Keep your numbers low if you want a good meeting.

In preparing for the meeting, think through how you will present your argument. Prepare a one-page hand out for the decision-maker, setting out your case very succinctly. Decision-makers are likely to have received a briefing note in advance from their staff. At the level of a cabinet member at the provincial, state or federal level, this is a certainty. The likelihood is that departmental staff has prepared a note explaining why your demand cannot be met. By preparing your own note, you may be able to counter the advice that likely tells the politician why she should ignore your views.

Prepare your note with an opening paragraph describing the problem. Include a middle section for discussion of the issue, stressing your view of the problem. The last paragraph should set out clearly what you want the decision-maker to do. Use headings: "Problem," "Discussion," "Solution." The "solution" is your request.

Believe it or not, the "ask," the clear statement of exactly what your group wants, is frequently overlooked as groups prepare to meet with a decision-maker. It is easy to get lost in the details, or overwhelmed by the struggle. Anger at the indifference of government, side issues and digressions, should not be allowed to overwhelm your meeting. The planning that goes into your specific request is particularly helpful in ensuring you are asking the decision-maker to do something within their power. If you are meeting with another member of the government and want her help to encourage the actual decision-maker, you need to ask for that help, not for a decision that is not hers to make. By writing out your briefing note, you can help keep your meeting on track. Furthermore, if you hand your one-pager to the minister as the meeting begins, she may begin using your note to scribble her own notes. The page will go into the file for use in recalling the details of the meeting.

The last bit of preparation is background research about the decision-maker. You should know as much as you can about the person you will be meeting. Did she live in a community in which you once lived? Did she go to school with your mother? You will break down some barriers right away if there are such common bonds. Is there anything in their background that suggests an interest in your issue? Has the individual ever done anything helpful on an environmental issue? There is no better way to start a meeting than by thanking the politician for something he has done in the past. It does not matter how long ago it was. That decision-maker is sure that everyone should know about his or her great record, even if no one remembers.

THE MEETING ITSELF

Obvious points, but worth mentioning: 1) Plan to be early to avoid arriving late. 2) Dress appropriately: suits, no jeans. Look professional. (I even wear make-up for meetings. I think of it as "war paint.")

The more powerful the person you are meeting, the more likely it is that your meeting will start late. Stay calm and patient. When your meeting does start, be sure to double-check how much time is available for the meeting. You want to be sure to have time in the meeting for the politician's reaction. You do not want to chew up the whole meeting haranguing the politician without getting feedback.

As in every social human contact, start with introductions. Do not rush through the small talk. Many politicians (and members of society as a whole) have a caricature of an activist in their minds. It is not a pretty picture. They may be expecting a one-dimensional zealot; someone from another planet. Time spent at the outset establishing the fact that your little group is a fine and *normal* group of constituents is important.

Once you are all settled in for the actual discussion, and you have double-checked how long the politician has to meet with you, set out one last important ground rule: let the politician know that you hope the meeting will be "off the record." Be clear that you have no intention of repeating anything she says in the meeting to the media. Some groups make the mistake of alerting the media to the fact of the meeting and that your group will meet with the press immediately afterward. Once the politician is aware of this, the meeting will never get past reiterations of whatever has been previously stated publicly. Worse yet, if the politician does not know you are planning to meet with the media, you will have sandbagged him. You will very rightly earn his ire. You are unlikely to ever re-establish a working relationship. In the same vein, for heaven's sake, do not plunk a tape recorder on the table if you want to create a collaborative atmosphere!

On the other hand, once you have set out your intention to keep the meeting off the record, you may get some useful information. Go through your pitch clearly and logically. Always stop and answer questions from the politician. If you do not know the answer to a question, do not bluff. Be honest. Tell her you do not know the answer, but will get the information and send it to her as soon as possible. (And be very sure to do so!)

Be sure to leave at least fifteen minutes for discussion. You should close your presentation by asking very directly for help, and/or advice. You may find the politician is actually more or less on your side but has other obstacles within cabinet. If he says, "Can you shift some of your letter-writing from my office over to the Minister of Finance? Unless I get her on board, I'll never be able to get the rest of cabinet," that is both very useful and very confidential information.

If the entire response from the politician is defensive and argumentative, try not to interrupt. Try to hear him out. Try to summarize the concerns dispassionately: "So, what we are hearing is that if we could address the economic problems of this region and find a viable alternative for this hazardous waste facility, you would be open to that?" Do everything you can to be diplomatic and create some room for dialogue.

If the politician is just plain flat-out misinformed, assume that you are being helpful by making him aware of that. In other words, de-personalize your reply. Never say, "You are wrong!" Say, "We have been concerned that some of the flawed information from the industry has been fed into your department. We would be happy to provide you with the independent scientific analysis that clearly establishes that the information your department has given you is outdated."

As your meeting winds up, be sure to make a note of, and repeat, any commitments you have made to the politician and any promises that have been made to you. Thank the politician. On the way out, thank any support staff you can. If you brought literature on your issue, be sure to share it with the staff as well.

OPPOSITION PARTIES

Do not forget to brief the Opposition and seek its support. Someday the Opposition critics may be government. In the meantime, if you can get the Opposition to champion your cause, you have succeeded in raising the issue in both the media and political calculation. The worst thing a social change group can do is to be overly friendly with the government in power and forget the Opposition. The Toronto-area environmental movement did this when the New Democratic government of Bob Rae was in power in Ontario. The green groups were so sure that Rae and his cabinet were their friends, that they blunted their own criticisms. They cut the Rae government too much slack and they ignored the Opposition. The result was predictable. The government took the environmental movement for granted. The next government assumed that the environment was not an issue that mattered to its supporters. The U.S. greens made the same mistake when Bill Clinton and Al Gore were in power. They didn't push ratifying Kyoto because they knew that the Democratic administration couldn't get Kyoto through Congress. As a result, when Bush reneged on Kyoto, hardly any of the environmentally literate public even knew its implications.

A social-change movement cannot afford to be partisan. Ever.

MEETING FOLLOW-UP

Always write a thank-you letter. In your letter, enclose any information you promised. Bear in mind that your letter to a provincial, state, or federal cabinet member is *not* a private document. Unless hand-delivered and marked "personal and confidential," it will be filtered down to the correspondence unit of the department and directed to the civil servant whose job it is to prepare a reply.

Even the most important letters will be diverted into the routine pipeline. Once, when I worked in the federal Minister of the Environment's office, Monte Hummel of the World Wildlife Fund phoned to ask if we had not been amazed by the personal letter to the minister from H.R.H. Prince Philip, the Duke of Edinburgh. "What letter?" It turned out a hand-typed letter, prepared by royalty on Buckingham Palace stationery, was already in the bowels of the department. When retrieved, it was already marred with a red ink date stamp "Received, Feb. 7, 1987" on top of the embossed Buckingham Palace letterhead.

As many eyes will see your letter, do not repeat anything confidential or sensitive. Do not write, "Thanks so much for letting us know you agree with us that the prime minister is a problem." *Do* reiterate any promises made: "Thank you for your commitment to release the draft guidelines for 'no net loss' of wetlands to us as soon as possible. We look forward to receiving them." Think of your letter as a jungle telegraph. Your letter to the minister lets the department know of any promises and will help make sure they are honoured.

I loved this story from a colleague of mine in government. His boss was the Minister for Indian and Northern Affairs. In checking the follow-up correspondence from a chief who had recently met with the minister, with this aide present, he realized that the chief's letter thanked the minister for a promise that had not been made in their meeting. It turned out the chief had, *for years*, written a thank-you letter after meeting with various ministers in which he thanked the minister for a commitment for thirty thousand dollars for the band council-office renovations, or fifteen thousand dollars to refurbish the community hall. Diligent bureaucrats had dispatched the cheques without any other evidence that the promise had been made.

Which brings us to the next lobbying target: the bureaucrat.

CIVIL SERVANTS

Many activists forget how powerful the unelected ranks of the bureaucracy can be in making decisions on critical issues. The ranks of the civil service watch political leaders and governing parties come and go like the tides. Some administrations may inflict lasting damage on their departmental goals. (Bush's trashing of the Environmental Protection Agency is a case in point.) But for the most part, the ship of state is steered by the bureaucracy. Government-wide objectives can remain remarkably unchanged by changes in government. Deputy ministers have a lot of power.

Unlike politicians, bureaucrats are largely invisible and often unaccountable. Bureaucrats do share a number of traits with politicians. They want to stay in power and for civil servants this means staying invisible. They do share the escalating scale of the power-accessibility ratio. The more powerful they are, the harder they are to reach. The good news is that the less-powerful civil servants are often very easy to meet. Often, they are kindred spirits; people who have studied the environment, care about nature, have sought a job in the area, and ended up in government. These are people who may want to help you.

Develop and cultivate these relationships. You could be rewarded with helpful brown envelopes.[19]

At least, you will find out what is really going on. Who is blocking progress on a key issue? Is it the politician? Or is it the senior bureaucracy?

When the civil service is the problem, you need to let the political staff know that. When you want action from a governmental official, letter-writing will not influence her in the same way it moves a politician. You may need a new tactic.

There is one cardinal rule: a citizen's group should never criticize a bureaucrat by name in a letter to the political masters. It is considered very bad form and results only in both civil service and politicians closing ranks to defend the external criticisms.

The queen of guerrilla tactics that move the bureaucracy is Love Canal's heroine, Lois Gibbs. Many people remember Love Canal, the toxic neighbourhood in upstate New York. Hooker Chemical's hazardous dump was seeping into basements, making children sick. People may remember that President Jimmy Carter acted to evacuate the subdivision, move and compensate families, and created the Superfund Program to cleanup toxic sites across the U.S. What people tend to forget is that Gibbs and the other distraught mothers of the neighbourhood had to take an EPA official hostage before action was taken.

Gibbs and her guerilla moms had more subtle tactics. When going in to meet a senior EPA official for the first time, they wanted to be sure he would do what they wanted. They wanted to be polite and winning, but be remembered as a group he would never want coming back to bother him. To achieve this delicate balance, the women brought their children. The children were told to be very good and very quiet. Gibbs and her friends gave each child a chocolate bar while they waited for the meeting to begin. The children were told they could eat the bar during the meeting, but had to stay very quiet. The moms and kids entered an inner sanctum of EPA's regional head. The furniture was elegant, with couches of white leather. Good as gold, each child eagerly, quietly opened the chocolate bars, now slightly warm and gooey from the heat of eager and patient hands. Alarm spread across the bureaucrat's face as chocolatey fingers came perilously close to his pristine furniture. The moms, acting oblivious to the chocolate menace, explained the toxic threat to their children's health.

You have to be creative in thinking through your own strategy. I have personally never used chocolatey kids to terrorize a bureaucracy. I have, on the other hand, had lots of lobbying experiences involving carrying my infant daughter into meetings. This was not a tactic; it was life. It definitely humanized me and reduced the impact of the activist label. I didn't seem so dangerous when carrying a three-month-old baby. (This was particularly true for making contacts in industry.) I can remember turning to check on where the baby was when giving testimony to a House of Commons committee. The friend who had been holding her was empty-handed. He passed me a note to quell any worries. It turned out one of the MPs had decided she wanted to stroll a bit walking with the baby. My daughter was fourteen days old when she met her first cabinet minister, the minister responsible for national parks. A grandmother herself, the minister had a baby gift for me at our meeting. (Now that was a first!) Nursing presented very few problems, whether in seeing Bill Clinton in the Oval Office, Prince Charles on the Royal Yacht *Britannia*, or having dinner with then Liberal environment critic Paul Martin in the Parliamentary Dining Room. (Although, when I asked Martin if he thought anyone would mind if I nursed the baby, he did look as though I'd put an electric shock into the cushion of his chair. "Mind? Why would anyone mind?" he said in an attempt to subdue his own discomfort. Looking nervously around the dining room, he did his best to relax about the prospect, "I mean, it's perfectly natural. Why would anyone mind?" When she'd finished nursing, a waitress came and asked if she could walk a bit with the baby. Martin did finally relax, and became rapturous about women, "Aren't women wonderful? A man wouldn't have thought to come and offer to walk the baby.") While bringing a baby is not a lobbying ploy, it does not hurt. And carrying a baby is definitely a magnet for media. Anti-nuclear activist Dr. Helen Caldicott used to say that in campaigning, "If you have a baby, bring her. If you don't have a baby, have one. If you can't have a baby, borrow one!"

THINK

Pay attention to the power structure. Watch whose career (political or civil service) is on the rise. With whom should we meet? How can we be helpful, even to those people who are not running for office?

Lobbying bureaucrats and politicians is just like local community organizing. Find your allies. Cultivate them. Network. Share information. Figure out who knows whom. Find the people who play golf with the minister, who go to church with the deputy minister. Find the people who run into the premier's wife at parties. Have these people raise the issues. Feed their impressions of what is really going on back into your planning strategy. Leave no stone unturned.

THE THANK YOU

One of the major gripes from politicians about environmental and social-change groups is that we are never satisfied. This is likely true. There is always more that needs to be done. However, we should do everything possible to reverse the unhelpful perception that, no matter what a politician does for an environmental group, we won't vote for their party (all three major parties in Canada increasingly think this), and that they will not get any credit for doing the right thing.

When you win (and by now I hope you know you will win), be sure to thank any politician who helped. A letter of thanks is the minimum expression of gratitude. Far better is a public recognition. This really sends a positive signal to those who doubted there was any political benefit for protecting the environment. Put out a press release congratulating the decision-maker. It is highly likely that the release will receive zero coverage. A green group thanking a politician for saving a forest is the classic non-story for reporters. Do it anyway, but be sure to send the release to the office of the person you are praising. They may not see it otherwise.

There are also awards you can give. They do tend to get media coverage. Be creative.

Send valentines. Have children make a big, colourful, thank-you banner. Send flowers. (Tell the florist to send locally grown cut flowers or plants with roots to avoid supporting pesticide poisonings in Colombian floral workers!)

If you know a politician well enough to like them and read in the paper that they have just lost a parent, send a note. They are no different than any normal person. It will matter to them.

How do you thank a bureaucrat? Press releases are not on. So do something personal. A simple "thank you" is often a surprise. Once, an environmental official released a really brave report with clear data exposing pollution. Sure, it was his job, but it was also clear and uncompromising. I looked up his home phone number and left a message expressing gratitude and admiration. I found out much later that the family saved the recorded message. They were really pleased and he was quite moved. It took me less then three minutes to register that little thank you. Who knows how much difference it may have made?

Lobbying is not a short-term effort. Like all the aspects of campaigning, you may be in this for the long haul. Be fair. Be empathetic. But do not compromise on the ultimate goal.

WHEN THE GOVERNMENT COMES TO YOU: PUBLIC CONSULTATION

There is another way in which you will be interacting with government. Public consultation exercises are common. Most are a sham. There used to be more genuine opportunities for expressing public concerns through public hearings and meetings. Thirty years ago, the government (local, provincial, state or national) would hold a meeting with presenters and then accept questions from the audience. This was a form of direct democracy. The consultations were like town hall meetings.

Recently, the consultations have been taken over by consultants. The communications consultants working for government and industry promise to manage public engagement. Now, meetings convened by government as public consultation are more likely to be "open houses." An open house has as much relation to a public consultation as a straitjacket does to wings.

The open house is all about control. There is no public meeting. Citizens are to wander through a set of exhibits where someone allegedly knowledgeable is available at each station. In the good old-fashioned public meeting, if one person had good questions, everyone in the hall heard them. If the so-called expert had pathetically weak answers, everyone heard those as well. Not so in the open house. No one's questions are heard by an audience. No audience, in fact, is ever formed. Mingling replaces assembling. Public concern is managed and shut down.

If you are presented with a series of open houses masquerading as public consultation, denounce the process immediately. Ask the responsible minister to hold a genuine consultation. Ask that the intermediary layer of professional communications consultants be removed. Taxpayers' dollars are spent in large amounts to defeat true public engagement. We need to end this absurdity.

Hold your own public meetings. Invite the same government and industry experts. Invite your own as well.

LOBBYING THE CORPORATION

Yes, it is possible to lobby a corporation, but, as noted, it is an "unnatural person" and none of the above applies.

There are two major ways to influence corporate behaviour: shareholder actions and boycotts.

1) If you can buy a single share in a corporation, you are entitled to attend shareholder meetings. You can speak out against policies that are destructive, to human rights or the environment. Alerting the media that there will be a protest at a shareholders meeting can yield effective results. Corporations care about reputation. Shareholder actions in divesting holdings in South Africa were a significant factor in ending apartheid.

2) Boycotts: Widespread consumer boycotts can be effective. As noted earlier, the "Boycott Grapes" campaign was ultimately successful. A smart corporation like McDonald's will yield to a boycott campaign

before it can impact their bottom line as it does not want to risk its relationship with its consumers.

The farther the company is from the retail level, the more removed from the individual consumer, the more sophisticated your campaign must be. Groups like Forest Ethics have perfected the "markets" campaign. Clayoquot Sound veteran, Tzeporah Berman (now with Forest Ethics), targets lingerie retailer Victoria's Secret for buying paper from a pulp and paper company that conducts unsustainable boreal forest clear-cuts, which threaten the survival of woodland caribou. The paper supplier is too far from the consumer to feel the wrath of green buyers, but the big catalogue purchasers are not. Markets campaigns have shifted big companies like Home Depot to a greener purchase policy for forest products. Markets campaigns work best when there is a sustainable certified alternative, such as Forest Stewardship Council forest products, certified organically grown produce, or Marine Stewardship Council sea food.

CONCLUSION

Any well-organized citizens' group can influence government policy in a democracy. It is not very complicated. You just have to believe in your right to speak out. And you have to be willing to expect the best from the people you elect.

LESSONS LEARNED:

1) You can meet anyone you need to meet.
2) Cultivate the gatekeepers.
3) Do your homework—on your issue and the person you want to influence.
4) Leave no stone unturned.
5) Talk to everyone you can in the "system."
6) Always keep your word. Keep any shared confidences confidential.
7) Do not bluff. If you do not have the answer, say so.
8) Never, ever, be rude.
9) Treat politicians as you would want to be treated. This obviously means no custard pies, unless they are for dessert.
10) Be fair. Be polite. Take no prisoners.

Chapter 9

USING THE COURTS

THERE ARE BASICALLY THREE WAYS an activist ends up in court: by suing a polluter or a government, by getting arrested, or being sued by a polluter. None of these is any fun.

SUE THE BASTARDS

A book by this name by a grassroots activist suggested the way to success for the environmental movement lay in taking polluters to court.[20] Not surprisingly, the book was written by an American for a U.S. audience. This is one area of activist training where the advice is very different between Canada and the United States.

I write this as a "lawyer in recovery." I was once a practising lawyer, was called to the bar in two provinces, and appeared at provincial and federal court levels. I actually loved being a lawyer. I even loved law school.

Having gone to law school to practise environmental law, I was severely disappointed to realize Canada didn't have any. Many of my friends practising environmental law in Canada will howl in protest at this blanket statement. Of course, I am exaggerating to make a point, but only slightly. Canada has a number of laws to protect the environment, but they create very little access to the courts for concerned citizens. And Canadian courts are loathe to question the judgment of cabinet ministers.

The situation is quite different in the United States. There, that well-known eco-radical president, Richard M. Nixon, brought in a slew of tough laws: the Clean Air Act, the Clean Water Act, the National Environmental Protection Act, the Endangered Species Act. These laws have been used time and time again by environmentalists in the U.S. These laws have led the judiciary to intervene to protect endangered species and eroding shoreline, to stop dams and to punish toxic dumpers.

Canada has laws, but there are very few citizen enforcement mechanisms. Trying to use common law, or the traditions of age-old British justice, is even more uphill.

In 1982, seventeen of us in Nova Scotia tried to use the old common-law causes of action of trespass and nuisance to stop the planned spraying by pulp-and-paper companies of forested areas near our homes with the fifty-fifty mixture of phenoxy herbicides 2,4-D and 2,4,5-T that was known as Agent Orange in Vietnam.[21] We were lucky in gaining an interim injunction that prevented the spraying from taking place until our case could be heard on its merits. I was in law school and worked on the case pretty much full-time through third year law. The trial was a month long. Despite expert testimony from some of the most prestigious medical experts and scientists from around the world, we lost. The case cost us over two hundred thousand dollars—money we raised through quilt raffles and bake sales and appeals to caring people across Canada. During a preliminary legal skirmish, my family lost eighty acres of land overlooking the Bras D'Or Lakes to pay off a court-ordered bill to Scott Paper. The pulp company lawyers used every procedural maneuver to break us financially. I got the lecture in the bar admission course: if you are representing a client with deep pockets and the other side is impecunious, wear them down; break them financially. This isn't even considered sneaky; it's recognized as good representation of your client.

All told, the case took two years, as though the time had been vacuumed. It was the most painful chapter of my life and I will likely never be completely over it. The judge ruled that Agent Orange was safe. He even ruled it had never caused any problems in Vietnam. And then he ordered that the plaintiffs in the herbicide case should pay the pulp company's court costs. The PR spokeswoman (of course, the industry always hires women to be their media voice), estimated their costs at over one million dollars. People began to crack. We were forced into an out-of-court settlement. The case was never appealed.

Charles Dickens summarized my experience in *Bleak House*:

This is the Court of Chancery, which has its decaying houses and its blighted lands in every shire, which has its worn-out lunatic in every madhouse and its dead in every churchyard, which has its ruined suitor with his slipshod heels and threadbare dress borrowing and begging through the round of every man's acquaintance, which gives to monied might the means abundantly of wearying out the right, which so exhausts finances, patience, courage, hope, so overthrows the brain and breaks the heart, that there is not an honourable man among its practitioners who would not give—who does not often give—the warning, 'Suffer any wrong that can be done you rather than come here!'[22]

Or as one of my law professors used to say, "Your client does not want to be a leading case."

Following the herbicide case, I developed an undifferentiated fear of men in suits at the end of any block in downtown Halifax. It might be one of the lawyers for the pulp company or, worse yet, the judge who held himself out as the world's leading expert on phenoxy herbicides. I'd freeze, break into a sweat and only relax once I was close enough to tell for sure. Once the judge did bump into me. He was so frazzled he dropped a bunch of stuff at my feet. I froze, but I can still recall the image. My new shoes so close to his face. I moved to Ottawa.

Going to court may be necessary, but it should be your last resort.

"I WANT MY DAY IN COURT!"

Citizens' groups often gravitate to the courts. They are looking for justice and hope to find it there. What they often do not realize is that the decision to go to court creates nearly unbearable pressures on small citizens' groups. The negative impacts on your organization include:

- Once you hire a lawyer, the lawyer does not want to deal with dozens of people. The lawyer will, quite logically, insist on a small group of people with authority to give her instructions. This winnowing down of decision-makers is antithetical to maintaining strong volunteer energies;
- Unless you have been very fortunate and found a lawyer willing to act *pro bono* (not billing for his time as the case is in the public interest), or have found an environmental law group willing to provide legal counsel at no charge[23], your group will quickly find that going to court is very expensive. Money-raising will become your number one

group activity. Even with *pro bono* legal services, disbursements must be paid. And, in Canada, there is the added financial risk of having court costs awarded against you in the event you lose;

- Your media campaign could become constrained. Your lawyer may want you to avoid news coverage that could annoy the judge in the case;
- Politicians will take the fact of a court case as an "out." Elected officials are only too happy to avoid comment, intoning meaningfully that "the matter is before the courts."

So with all these downsides, should a Canadian citizens' group ever go to court? The answer is a resounding yes, if the following questions can be answered in the affirmative:

- Do you have a strong legal argument? No lawyer can ever promise success, but going to court as a *beau geste* is a huge mistake. Only if you have a reasonably good chance of success, should you go for it.
- Have you exhausted all other remedies? Perhaps there are still political decisions that can be influenced more easily than by resorting to the courts.
- Is the damage to the environment imminent and irreversible? If so, going to court, either by seeking an injunction—or ending up there for blockading the threatened action—may be your only hope.

This brief chapter is not intended to give you a crash course in environmental law, but still, a quick review of key concepts could be helpful.[24]

The most productive area of Canadian environmental litigation is in a branch of law called administrative law. This area allows courts to rule on the fairness of government action. If a law sets up a process for citizen engagement, and the public is denied a reasonable opportunity to participate, that is a likely case for Canadian court intervention. Similarly, if a law sets out projects and decisions that require an environmental assessment, and the government decision-maker avoids such assessment, the courts will intervene to say the government must go back to square one and do an assessment.

In other words, Canadian courts will intervene to ensure the letter of the law is observed. Canadian courts do not want to be seen as *making* new law, unless the issue is one where the courts must interpret, such as in human rights cases under the Charter of Rights and Freedoms.

The remedies open to the courts in administrative law are helpful, but always fall short of complete victory. A common remedy is *certiorari*—an order to the minister to quash a previous decision (such as a permit) if it was made based on a flawed process. The original outcome is not attacked on its merits, but as a matter of procedure.

What happens if you win? Generally, the government then will go back, redo the process, avoiding earlier procedural errors, and come out with the same decision as it did initially. Another weakness of the Canadian process is that even as a law suit is launched claiming that a project requires environmental review, construction can continue.

The most famous case in Canadian environmental jurisprudence of an activist chasing a project through the courts is the Old Man Dam. Alberta veterinarian and stalwart environmentalist Dr. Martha Kostuch took the fight against the dam on the Old Man River all the way to the Supreme Court of Canada. It took five years and, despite lawyers working for vastly reduced fees, cost over a hundred thousand dollars. The Supreme Court finally ruled that the Old Man Dam could not be built without an environmental assessment first. Unfortunately, the ruling came after the dam was completed, so the court's remedies lay in on-going monitoring and water-level controls, many of which were never implemented.

Despite the weaknesses of the remedies, the ability of environmental groups to force ministers to reverse decisions and start over has been a strategic advantage in numerous Canadian cases.

The situation is different in the United States. Some of the downsides still apply,[25] but U.S. courts have historically been far more willing to second-guess government decision-makers. The financial risks are reduced as costs are not awarded against public interest groups. As well, the practice of taking cases on a contingency basis, in which a lawyer agrees to charge nothing in exchange for taking a share of the proceeds of a successful outcome, while unusual in Canada, is quite common in the U.S. The rules for class actions are easier.

Nevertheless, even in the U.S., issues of scientific uncertainty are not well-handled in the legal system. In the best-seller *A Civil Action*, lawyer

Jan Schlichtmann took on an old toxic dump site in Woburn, Massachusetts.[26] On behalf of sick and worried families, he attempted to prove causation, linking the dumping to water contamination and a high level of cancers. The case led to financial ruin for Schlichtmann and smashed the hopes of the plaintiffs. (Remember: your client does not want to be a leading case). The story made a good movie, but it is *Erin Brockovich*, the movie and the dynamo personality, that people remember. Both Brockovich herself and Julia Roberts acting the part were fabulous. The image of a gorgeous woman in high heels sneaking onto utility company land to obtain toxic water samples could make environmental campaigning glamorous. In the end, in real life, a major corporation was forced to pay millions to the neighbours they had been poisoning with chromium 6. The kind of directed court decision that led to justice for California plaintiffs in that case is not universally available in the U.S., and not at all in Canada.

Whether you are in the U.S. or Canada, before you decide to go to court, get more than one legal opinion. Interview lawyers willing to take your case (after first verifying that the initial consultation will be at no charge). Recognize that if you win on the first round, the other side is likely to appeal to a higher court. If you lose, you may also want to appeal but your financial situation will always be more precarious than that of the government or corporation you are fighting.

Be prepared when you go to court. Have your eyes wide open. In advance, work through how your group will avoid the many stresses the lawsuit will create within your organization. Once you take the plunge, always remember to stay in control. The lawyer works for you; not the other way around. Insist on clear information. When there is a choice to be made (appeal or don't appeal, challenge their preliminary motion or accept it, etc.), do not be rushed into giving instructions to your lawyer. Make sure you have a complete picture of the pros and cons and try to keep your entire grassroots group thoroughly involved.

GETTING ARRESTED: THE CIVIL DISOBEDIENCE OPTION

From Henry David Thoreau to Gandhi, non-violent civil disobedience has a long and respectable tradition. Rosa Parks, Martin Luther King, and even former Ontario premier Bob Rae who as Opposition leader was arrested on a logging road in Temagami, Ontario, have in common deciding that a higher law compelled them to break the current rules of the state. Many environmental campaigns have included civil disobedience, most commonly the use of blockades—whether against logging trucks or bulldozers.

The initial choice to block a road on public land is not necessarily illegal. However, once the logging company or contractor goes to court and obtains an injunction against such activities, presence on the road is illegal. The police may be brought in to haul protesters to jail. The charge is no longer trespass, but contempt of court. As noted, in the summer of 1993, dubbed Clayoquot Summer, over eight hundred people were arrested on the logging roads at Clayoquot Sound. Many did significant jail time. The government decided to treat the peaceful protesters as guilty of criminal contempt, instead of mere civil contempt. The result was sentences longer than those for first offenders for drug charges or some violent crimes. Those like Betty Krawczyk, a grandmother from Victoria, who refused to sign a promise to stay away from the road, spent months in jail.

Krwaczyk explained the legal process, admitting that she had become something of an expert in injunctions:

> Judges have ruled in the past that a charge of civil contempt changes to criminal contempt based on how public the protest is…. Since attracting public attention (and hopefully support for one's cause) is one of the main reasons for civil disobedience, the citizen who decides to put his or her body on the line is almost certain to be charged with criminal contempt of court. But when the charge is elevated to criminal contempt, this doesn't mean that you will then have the protection of the Criminal Code. Oh, no. All it means is that your punishment will be harsher. It is still contempt of court, so the provisions of the Criminal Code don't apply. In other words, a murderer can have his or her reasons for murdering someone taken into account by a judge, but an anti-logging protester does not have that right.[27]

When I visited Krwaczyk at the Nanaimo jail during her first four-month prison term, her guards told me she was a model prisoner. What else would one expect from a well-read, deeply committed, environmental-activist grandmother? I asked her what the worst part of jail time was for her. She mused about the stress of being away from family and expressed much more concern for some of her fellow inmates. Some of the women were young and had been unprepared for the idea of doing any jail time at all. Krwaczyk was quite sure about the worst part. "I really don't like my computer classes," she grinned mischievously, "They have programs to make sure we can be valuable to society. They are making me learn Word Perfect and I really hate it."

At the time, I thought her chances of recidivism were very low. I was wrong. In 2000, she was arrested protesting the logging of the Elaho Valley, and particularly a violent attack on protesters by pro-logging thugs. The attack was video-taped, but no charges were ever brought against the perpetrators. For Krwaczyk's crime of peacefully blocking the road, she was sentenced to a full year in jail.[28]

If you decide to engage in civil disobedience as one of your campaign strategies, be prepared to accept the consequences of your actions. This is one of the *sine qua nons* of a deeply rooted and moral action. The action of the state in jailing people—people who have not endangered anyone, nor harmed anyone, but have simply broken an unjust law in order to expose that injustice—is a powerful shaming mechanism. As Betty Krawczyk wrote, "I welcomed a harsh sentence because the very harshness immediately threw into bold relief the inherent injustice of how British Columbia's justice system deals with citizens who dare to directly challenge logging corporations."[29]

The more people the state puts in jail, the more the state loses face. Of course, this approach only applies in a democracy with respect for civil liberties. It would be a hopeless strategy in Augusto Pinochet's Chile or General Sani Abacha's Nigeria. Ruthless dictators do not lose sleep over people of conscience rotting in their jails. Gandhi recognized this in choosing a strategy of civil disobedience to resist colonial rule in India. He observed that such a strategy would only work to influence people like the British because the British conceived of themselves as fundamentally decent. In other words, their consciences could be pricked.

As well, the government tried to jail one of the peace-camp organizers. Tzeporah Berman made a point of never violating the injunction. She stayed off the road, but was a key organizer of the protest effort. The notion that she was guilty of a conspiracy to show criminal contempt of court was certainly novel. The charges were thrown out of court by the judge in the first hearing, but not until Berman had endured months of worry and fear for her future.

Before you decide to break the law to protect the environment, be sure you have no other choice. Be sure you have exhausted all the legal mechanisms of a democracy, met every politician, talked to every reporter, and see no hope of change. If it is truly your last resort, non-violent civil disobedience is an honourable choice.[30]

In the current climate of terrorist panic and the infringements on civil liberties, civil disobedience has extra risks. Any decision to break the law can be escalated into confrontation far more readily than in the pre–September 11 climate. This is compounded by the relatively new problem of lawbreakers who are not interested in being non-violent, nor in facing consequences.

The peaceful marches in November 1999 at the meeting of the World Trade Organization in Seattle were disrupted by crowbar-wielding, masked agitators. Some may accept that they were young, politically disenchanted idealists. For myself, I think they were *agent provocateurs.* None were arrested, although they roved freely smashing plate glass windows in the downtown. Only other protesters attempted to stop them. The police watched impassively. Within hours, there were curfews and tear gas, percussion grenades and a shift from local police to national guardsmen in riot gear. Whatever the motives of the black outfitted vandals, their actions turned the streets into a police state.

Having taken part in demonstrations of all kinds—marches, rallies and vigils—for over forty-six years, I had never encountered anything like the so-called anarchists of Seattle. I was tear-gassed at the Chicago Democratic Convention in 1968, but there the police action had been entirely unprovoked. As the official report determined, the 1968 Chicago chaos was due to a "police riot."

Since 1968, I have always known that the fabric of a democratic state and respect for the citizenry's right to free assembly and freedom of speech can vanish as quickly as Mayor Daley can order the police to the streets, or as a prime minister can invoke the War Measures Act.[31] I had never imagined that the movement for social justice, for environmental protection, and for peace on earth, would itself condone violence in its midst.

In fairness, most elements of the anti-globalization movement have urged only non-violent civil disobedience. Nevertheless, there is, in my view a well-meaning but naive willingness to tolerate the property-smashers. The slogan for acceptance has a tolerant ring. We are told we must accept "diversity of tactics." We are told that with all the pain and suffering in the world, with the egregious wrongs visited on the weak by the strong, with the obscene actions of transnational corporations, how can we condemn those who resort to the relatively small gesture of breaking a McDonald's window?

Easily. We have to condemn their actions. I condemn them on two grounds. The first is moral. We cannot risk becoming the monster we want to defeat. We cannot lose our souls or become hateful. We should never do to another human being that which we would not want done to ourselves. Gandhi, Martin Luther King, and Thoreau would never have condoned violence.

The second ground, which would also have been immediately recognized by Gandhi and King, brilliant strategists and campaigners that they were, is that these tactics are completely ineffective. They are counterproductive. They undermine the whole movement. These tactics alienate the watching public, on their couches in their living rooms, who have no idea what the message is. All they can see is hoodlums. When the G-8 was in Genoa, hundreds of thousands gathered. Months of work by a vast coalition of NGOs representing all the key issues of human rights, environment, development, and globalization had worked to ensure a well-organized, peaceful event. But then the so-called anarchists showed up. Someone died. The event was remembered for the violence. A key organizer, Susan George, named what the anarchists were: opportunists, free-riders who took advantage of everyone else's efforts to play out a different scenario. At the Live 8 demonstrations in Edinburgh in July 2005, the appearance of people in face masks, smashing things, was immediately denounced by Sir Bob Geldof. He had no problem worrying about "diversity of tactics." He condemned them as a bunch of "losers."

Canadian lawyer Clayton Ruby knows the score. In planning meetings before the Free Trade Area of the Americas Summit in Quebec City in April 2001, he was asked what to do if someone in your group wants to break the code of non-violence. What do you do if someone in your affinity group wants to talk about explosives? Ruby didn't hesitate. "You get a picture of them. You tell them you now suspect that they are under-cover working for the RCMP. You don't tolerate that sort of suggestion."

Do not think it is far-fetched to imagine someone, even in your own group, may be undercover for a law enforcement agency. It is actually near-fetched, especially if your group is prepared to consider direct-action tactics. Earth First founder Dave Foreman found out the hard way. He was awakened one morning, in bed with his wife, barrels of guns in their faces and a SWAT team in his bedroom. He was charged with conspiracy to blow up a dam. He was never convicted. The conspiracy charge was based on testimony of someone in the group. They had all felt sorry for him; a loser who kept saying maybe they should get explosives. They humoured him, with no interest in taking him up on his suggestion. He was working for the FBI.

In Canada, an RCMP agent burned down a barn in Quebec in an effort to prove his *bona fides* to a separatist group. Meanwhile in Alberta, the preacher and rancher turned anti-oil industry activist, Weibo Ludwig, was jailed on a conspiracy charge, based on a former friend, turned informer, with explosives provided by the police.

In my view, the movement must be far more self-disciplined. Violence is not acceptable. Period.

IS PROPERTY DESTRUCTION EVER DEFENSIBLE?

Is destruction of property always considered a violent act? Are there exceptions? Two exceptions must be noted: Jesus Christ and Captain Paul Watson.

Don't panic. I am not suggesting these two men are comparable. One was perfect, and the other is certainly not. (Believe me, Watson would be the first to confirm his imperfections.) I think the only commonality in the exception is this: both destroyed property directly related to and integral to the illegal act they found offensive. The destruction of property in both cases was not violence for its own sake. It was directed at the very equipment of immorality.

For Jesus, it was the moneylenders within the temple itself, and those with them who sold at exorbitant prices live animals for sacrifice. It was a scam. Worshippers were told they would please God with their sacrifice, but that only animals purchased inside the temple were acceptable. Jesus (whom I recognize as Lord, but who for non-Christians can at least be recognized as an historical figure and apostle of non-violence) did something extraordinary. He went into the temple and turned over the tables. And not nicely. It was clearly, in all Gospel descriptions, an alarming, direct and violent act. Property, such as doves caged for sale and sacrifice, flew the coop. All the while Jesus decried what the money changers had done to the House of his Father. This is the same Jesus who said we should love our enemies, and if struck, turn our cheek to be struck again. He stopped his followers from raising weapons to protect him in the Garden at Gesemene when his life was in the balance. No one in human history more perfectly stands for non-violence. Yet, he smashed the tables of the moneylenders and sellers of sacrificial animals.

Captain Paul Watson and the Sea Shepherd Conservation Society have a policy of non-violence. But they have arranged for the sinking of vessels involved in illegal whaling activities as determined by the International Whaling Commission. They have never used explosives, but did scupper two whalers in Reykjavik Harbour. Having walked through the vessels to ensure no one was aboard, they opened the valves to let in the sea. A whaler tied up nearby was left alone when they found a sleeping watchman on board. I have asked Watson, what if they had missed someone? What if someone had been hurt? He always replies that we should judge them by their record. They have never hurt anyone. He is on thinner ice here, but so far, Sea Shepherd is injury-free. That does not include Watson, or his crew, of course, who have been beaten up and risked serious injury time and time again in their efforts to protect marine mammals.

Paul Watson is also very familiar with the inside of jail cells. His favourite for many years was the one in Cheticamp, Cape Breton, where he was held in 1983. They fed him take-out pizza with his choice of toppings and wheeled the television to his cell so he could watch his coverage. However, I suspect the jail in the Netherlands may be a new favourite. He was held on a warrant from Norway for the sinking of the *Nybraena* in 1992 for 120 days in 1997. One of the country's leading magazines described him as Holland's only political prisoner. The jail appreciated that he was vegetarian and gave him healthy food. He lost weight, had time to catch up on his reading, and the donations that poured in during his incarceration helped fund a new boat for Neptune's Navy, as the Sea Shepherd fleet is called.

Exhausting all other political and legal routes before resorting to a principled stand for illegal activity is essential. After forty thousand of us marched in Quebec City in the protests against an enlarged version of NAFTA for the Americas, I remember talking to a Parliamentarian who had not received a single letter from one of his constituents on the issue. Letter-writing seems boring compared with colourful marches, and running from tear gas. However, the latter would have been far more effective if everyone who participated had written several letters to MPS in the months leading to the summit.

The higher moral ground is the indispensable foundation for civil disobedience. Therefore, to be credible and to be effective, civil disobedience must be non-violent.

SLAPP SUITS

The last way in which activists find themselves in court is if they are sued. The practice of using frivolous law suits to shut down protest has become so common that it has a name: Strategic Litigation Against Public Participation (SLAPP).

SLAPP suits are a particularly nasty form of intimidation. As noted earlier in this chapter, any involvement with courts and lawyers is financially and emotionally draining. When you receive legal papers demanding thousands of dollars in damages for an alleged defamatory statement made by you personally or by your local group, the world falls in around you. Will you lose your home? How can you afford a lawyer? How long will this take?

These suits are especially common in Canada because our legal standards for libel and slander are far lower than in the U.S.

Far too many friends of mine have faced SLAPP suits designed to scare them and to punish them. In 1982, Dr. Donna Smyth, an English professor at Acadia University in Wolfville, Nova Scotia, was sued for libel based on an opinion piece she had written in the provincial daily. Smyth's article addressed the threat of uranium mining in Nova Scotia. The news-paper itself was not sued. This is always a clear sign of the intent to intimidate activists, and not to seek genuine damages from the publica-tion of a defamatory statement. She was shocked. The article was hardly libelous from her standpoint. Nevertheless, she was being sued by Dr. Leo Yaffe of McGill University. In the introductory paragraph of her opinion piece, Smyth had referred to the fact that Yaffe was making a pro-nuclear speaking tour of Nova Scotia. She wrote, "Dr. Leo Yaffe is one of the many 'experts' to be paraded before the Nova Scotia public in an effort to con-vince us uranium mining is safe." Yaffe alleged that the word "paraded" suggested he was in the pocket of the nuclear industry. Smyth saw two years of her life effectively destroyed. Hiring the lawyer, paying the lawyer, sleepless nights over whether she and her partner could hang on to the house and the goat farm where they lived.[32]

The actual trial was high theatre. Yaffe claimed his reputation had been damaged. Smyth's star witness, the indefatigable Dr. Ursula Franklin, was both a strong anti-nuclear scientific expert and also an old friend of Yaffe's. The jury melted as she explained that she had felt that what Yaffe had really needed after that article was a "nice hug." On cross-examination, Yaffe's lawyer lit into her, "Dr. Franklin, how would *you* feel if someone alleged that *you* were in the pocket of the nuclear industry?" In her perfect, but heavily German-accented, English, the retired profes-sor replied, "I rather think that in that case, it would be the nuclear industry that would sue."

The single most important decision Smyth made once in the jaws of the legal system was to insist on her right to a trial by jury.[33] It was clear from the judge's instructions to the jury that he thought they should find for the plaintiff, Yaffe. The jury found in favour of Smyth.

The cruelty of SLAPP suits is often missed by the public and the media. More recently, Bennett Environmental sued the Conservation Council of New Brunswick and two of its directors personally (David Coon and Inka Melewski) for statements about the potential health and environmental risks of the proposed toxic waste incinerator Bennett was building in northern New Brunswick. When Sierra Club of Canada issued a news release calling on the New Brunswick government to cover the legal costs for the environmental defendants,[34] a New Brunswick reporter called to quiz me as to why we were coming to Conservation Council's defense. "After all, if they aren't guilty of libel," he said, "they have nothing to worry about." I don't think he had ever considered the human element. The fact that Coon and his wife, Janice Harvey, were losing sleep (Would they lose their home if the case was lost? How could they pay their lawyer?) had simply never occurred to him.

There needs to be some form of legislation passed, similar to whistle-blower protection in the employment context, to protect those acting in the public interest who face lawsuits designed to SLAPP them down.

LESSONS LEARNED:

1) The courts are no fun for clients. They are only fun for lawyers.
2) Go to court only if it's a last resort.
3) Go to court only if you can win.
4) Plan ahead. Be prepared.
5) Stay in control; don't let your lawyer take over your case.
6) Civil disobedience is also a last-resort option.
7) Don't break the law unless you are prepared to go to jail.
8) There are no "get out of jail free" cards in real life.
9) Never condone violence in protests.
10) Only engage in non-violent civil disobedience.

Chapter 10

FUNDRAISING

IF THERE IS ONE INDISPENSABLE element to your campaign, it is not money. Far more important is your willingness to persevere, to be dogged and tireless. Your conviction that you can and will succeed is the most important part of any winning campaign. But, let's face it: money helps and you'll need it!

There is a natural conflict between effectiveness and wealth in environmental work, as well as in many social justice causes. As former Sierra Club (U.S.) executive director, the late David Brower used to say, "Any environmental group with money in the bank simply doesn't understand the severity of the problem."

In the beginning of most local campaigns, all the volunteer workers are also the main donors. I financed the early budworm-spray campaigns out of my waitressing tips. (Fortunately, I was a good waitress, and our campaign did not need much money!) There are many ways to support a campaign. Important donations can be of time, of loving moral support, and of money. Many environmental campaigns have been won without ever turning attention to fundraising plans and budgets. As soon as you realize your issue will not be won in a matter of weeks or months, the questions of finding and accounting for the money raised will require attention.

Like every other aspect of your effective work as an activist, good fundraising is all about building relationships: relationships with people who support your cause, relationships with staff in foundation and grant-making organizations, relationships with people in government who may operate citizen-funding programs. The essence of good fundraising comes down, once again, to those two magic words: "please" and "thank you."

THE SECRET OF RAISING MONEY

I will now share the big secret of successful fundraising (drum roll, please). To receive donations, you have to *ask*. This is actually harder than it sounds. Talking about money is something of a social *faux pas*. Asking a friend for a loan is so awkward; most people would rather go to a bank. Asking a friend for a donation to save a forest is a little easier, but not much. I continue to find it the hardest part of my work. Over time, the people who have been major donors to Sierra Club of Canada have also become some of my closest friends. (And some of my closest friends have become donors.) It is a miserable thing to have to ask ("What again!?") when other fundraising efforts have fallen short, or when the demands of the threats we are fighting exceed our bank account.

Back to my mother. The reason she was placed on Nixon's Enemies List was that she was a hugely successful fundraiser for candidates (generally Democrats) who opposed the Vietnam War. I think one reason we moved to Canada was that when she called people she genuinely adored to ask if they could come to dinner, they would ask, "And do I have to bring my chequebook? What's the cause this time?" She could only sputter her protestations of innocence—occasionally it really *was* just a dinner party.

Her fundraising efforts were amazing. They were all based on relationships, often with a heavy dose of celebrity attraction. She organized cocktail parties along Connecticut's Gold Coast, in homes in Westport, with Paul Newman as the guest attraction. (He is one of the nicest and most modest people I've ever met and he is also quite shy. I'll never forget Newman preparing to face a room full of people who adored him, standing in a corner, head bent toward the wall, while nervously chewing gum.) One fundraising party my mother organized for the 1972 McGovern for President campaign was at the Roxbury, Connecticut, home of novelist William Styron and his wife Rose, but invitations came from an array of "co-hosts" including Felicia and Leonard Bernstein, Arthur Miller and Inge Morath, and Cleve and Francine du Plessix Grey. They actually decided to make the dinner themselves for about one hundred people. Guests included sculptor Alexander Calder, Frederic March, and Florence Eldridge, as well as the Connecticut Democratic Party machine: John Bailey, and the vice-presidential candidate, and guest of honour, vice-presidential candiate Sargent Shriver.[36] My mom's fundraising pitch painted a grand picture of American youth losing faith in the American dream as she shared (catch in her throat) that her thirteen-year-old son had a picture of Che Guevara on his wall. Her plea for financial support brought tears to many eyes and caused Frederic March to tear up the first ten thousand-dollar cheque he had written and make out a new one, twice as large. This was in 1972. That was a lot of money then. And many guests wrote similar amounts. My job was to be her assistant, and in the car home, I'd ride shotgun and count up the night's total.

After every party, I also helped with the thank-you letters. She was always creative. The idea of a form letter would never have occurred to her. All donations were personally acknowledged. Sometimes we would receive a breathtakingly generous donation. She might send flowers in thanks. One time she asked me to use as many coloured markers as possible and draw bouquets of flowers for her thank-you notes. Another time I made a lot of seasonal valentines.

She never asked anyone to do more than she was prepared to do herself. In 1968, she needed thirty thousand dollars to print all the literature to kick off a primary campaign for Eugene McCarthy in Connecticut. She simply took out a second mortgage on our house. (Obviously it is important to have a supportive partner, as my dad always supported her volunteer campaigning.) When the literature arrived, it had nowhere to go but in our house. The boxes were piled to the ceiling and, for awhile, we were reduced to pathways through the living room and dining room. She would ride off to organize a town, taking literature with her, and gradually we got space in our house back. Within a short time, she had also fundraised back the money to pay off the second mortgage. She always used to say, "You have to spend money, to make money."

As I think over my life and work, I realize how much I've been influenced by her style. I also have mortgaged my house to cover initial costs (in that case it was to get the Kyoto ad in the *Globe and Mail*) and I always insist on signing every thank-you letter that goes out the door at Sierra Club of Canada, whether the donation is for five dollars or five thousand dollars. Nothing tells someone you appreciate, *truly appreciate*, their support, like a personalized thank you.

As you gear up for finding the financial support to win your campaign, you will discover there is a natural hierarchy of sources. There are several categories of fundraising efforts: individual donors, foundations, and governments. As Willie Sutton famously answered when asked why he robbed banks, "Because that's where the money is!"

RAISING MONEY: CANADA VERSUS THE U.S.

One of the worst fundraising lines I have ever heard was from the late Senator Edmund Muskie, speaking at a dinner to defray the deficit of Joe Duffey's 1970 failed run for the senate in Connecticut. Muskie, with a folksy Maine charm, may have thought it was funny when he said to a crowd of generous multiple-donors, "Contributors are like cows. They must be milked regularly and often." Ouch.

Statistics on philanthropy from Canada and the United States confirm that, in both countries, most charities' primary source of support is individual donors. Many, many small donations keep most community, environmental, human rights, public interest, and overseas development groups alive. In Canada, the relative percentage of one's income that is donated to charity goes up, as income goes down. In other words, our poorest citizens are the most generous.

This statistic has been translated into reality over and over again in my work. In 1981, when I was fundraising for Ethiopia Airlift,[36] the larger volume of donations, not just as a proportion of income but in actual dollars, came from Cape Breton Island. A wealthy South End Halifax resident felt that a twenty-five dollar donation was generous. On the other hand, from Glace Bay in industrial Cape Breton came a cheque for a thousand dollars. The accompanying note said, "I am a retired coal miner and this is all my savings, but those people need it more than I do."

Nationally, the donations for Ethiopia reflected that wealth was not a pre-condition for giving. As a proportion of income, the largest donations came from the Inuit in the far North who could actually recall famine conditions. The last famine in Canada had been in the late 1950s and people held the horror of it in living memory.

There are cultural differences between Canadian and American fundraising-styles. In the U.S., wealthy people are far more likely to make very large donations, even to more radical causes. Poor people give as well, but there is more of a tradition of largesse, *noblesse oblige* in the U.S. than Canada, aided by more sensible tax treatment to encourage philanthropy in the U.S.

Another problem for Canadian groups is the extent to which the general public assumes that all good causes receive large government support. People are often shocked to find that Sierra Club of Canada is not supported by the federal government. The reason is that so many other good causes are supported by the federal government. The Trudeau government started generous funding programs for development organizations, health advocacy, women's rights, consumer watchdogs, multicultural and social-justice advocates, and a host of others. No sector was excluded from funding, except the environmental movement. I think it was a blessing in disguise. Government money is drying up for the other sectors and that has created hardship. The environmental movement has had to be extremely lean and agile over the years. There was no chance of becoming complacent when you never knew where next month's payroll would come from. When the non-government organization (NGO) budget cuts started, a reporter asked me how Sierra Club of Canada was coping. I told him, "We are just like Cape Bretoners in the Depression. We never noticed, as we never had money in the first place."

Another big difference between Canada and the U.S. is that Americans expect a fundraising "pitch." They expect to be asked to take out their chequebook on the spot. There may be a challenge donation in the air in which some anonymous donor has promised to match every donation raised that evening. Most Canadians are far more uncomfortable with this approach. In fact, conventional philanthropic advice in Canada states that events, such as dinners and cocktail parties, should be pitch-free zones. You are supposed to gather everyone together, wine them and dine them, and phone later for the donation. I have had this experience at fundraisers for universities. Wanting to save time, I took out my chequebook and tried to make a donation to my law school at the end of the dinner. No one would take it. Sometimes I think conventional, professional fundraising advice in Canada is a crock.

You have to ask. You do not have to be aggressive or rude. You have to be passionate.

ARE YOU A CHARITY?

It is obvious that people are more comfortable and can make larger donations when they are donating to a registered charity. If you are a small citizens' group, chances are you are not a charity. As a practical matter, it is not possible to become one, at least not quickly. In Canada, registered charitable designations have become increasingly difficult to obtain. One option is to find a registered charity whose aims are consistent with yours and ask if they would be willing to accept donations you raise. It is perfectly legal to have an agency agreement, in which a group without charitable status receives funds raised through a charity. It does require that all the charitable rules of Canada and the U.S. are observed. In Canada, this means overt political advocacy can make up no more than 10 percent of your spending. Ultimately, the charity that agrees to take your group on as a project is responsible to the government for the proper management of charitable dollars. It is asking a lot, but a number of foundations may be willing to help you.

Whether with charitable donations or not, people will donate to support your work. You need to persuade them of the vital importance of your efforts. If you believe in your cause, and you have a track record that demonstrates you and your group are making a difference, you can raise money.

FUNDRAISING THROUGH COMMUNITY EVENTS

This is the logical place for fundraising, especially if your group does not have a charitable number. You can raise lots of money through events. Moreover, community events fulfill a number of goals for your group. A fundraising event raises public awareness of your issue. It lets the public know you need their support to do work they appreciate. An event provides a huge number of opportunities for volunteer engagement. An event also provides several good "media moments": announcing you plan to hold the event (with photo of organizing committee) and coverage of the actual events. You can invite local politicians, allowing them to align themselves publicly to your cause. Raising money through your fundraising event is actually only one of a number of important achievements.

Events allow you to play to your strengths and engage different segments of your community:

- Are there talented·local musicians who support your cause? You could hold a concert.
- A famous author? Ask her to do a reading or involve a number of authors in a literary event. Autographed copies of their books, can be auctioned.
- Do you know of local restaurateurs or chefs? A gourmet event with a high-ticket price can work.
- Local artists? An art auction can be part of a dinner or can be held on its own.
- Silent auctions with items donated from local businesses and supporters can bring in money, and engage a lot of you volunteer energy in collecting the items for an auction. You also increase the level of engagement of everyone who makes a donation.
- Donations for auctions can be for services. Ecology Action Centre in Halifax annually auctions things like a sail with member Rudy Haase, or a deluxe brunch at the home of another member. You do not have to count on access to priceless works of art. Swap babysitting offers or a family cottage for a week.
- In a rural area, a harvest-fair event with preserves and baked goods can be a lot of fun and a good fundraiser. A flea market can work. Entertain the kids with a clown, and face painting. One local Cape Breton fire brigade made extra money with a pie-throwing event featuring local celebrities. Sierra Club of Canada's local campaigner, Bruno Marccochio, brought in the most money.
- Make the event educational. Introduce knowledgeable wine tastings or hold cooking demonstrations with dining to follow.
- Run, walk, and roll races with participatory sponsorships work for the cancer groups (Run for the Cure), with those working to identify the causes of cancer (Running for Prevention).
- Hold a raffle for one amazing handmade quilt, or for a donated canoe. Raffles are not a one-time event, but also get the word out in your community and involve a lot of volunteer effort.

Be creative! There are as many ways to raise money in a community as there are interests, talents, and different cultures in your group. Significant amounts of money can be raised through these events. You should be able to make five thousand dollars easily and have the potential for thirty thousand dollars even in a relatively small community. When we were trying to raise money for the Altamira protest by Paiakan, in addition to the three concerts with Gordon Lightfoot, we invited people to a select cocktail party at a thousand dollars per couple to meet Margaret Atwood, Lightfoot, and Paiakan. That may seem a bit high-end, but it is nothing compared with World Wildlife Fund Canada's offer to woo one-million-dollar donors (and they had quite a few) to dinner at Buckingham Palace with H.R.H. Prince Philip. Celebrity contacts will help!

Do not leave the turn-out to chance. If you are holding an event where numbers really matter, you and your team will have to twist arms and work the phones. If it is two days before a dinner planned for sixty and you have only sold twenty tickets, feel free to share your sense of rising panic with the people you phone. Many a successful event was a looming disaster a few days before. Once, a friend chastised me at a glitteringly successful event. "You told me no one was coming! You said it was a disaster," he said. I answered truthfully, "It was when I phoned you!"

Schools and churches rely on community events for fundraising. If anyone was paying for staff time, these events would barely break even. It is the energy of the volunteers in your group that will make these events a success.

ALL DONORS BIG AND SMALL

Most people know a lot of other people. You may not think you know the "right" kind of people to raise a lot of money, but you undoubtedly know someone who does. Just as in reaching politicians you have asked ("Who knows someone who knows the premier's sister?") you need to figure out who knows the more wealthy people in your community. Prominent lawyers, doctors, and business people can all be reached. In the same way that the more powerful a politician is, the more gatekeepers will guard access; the wealthier someone is, the more hoops you have to go through. There is no better way to meet someone than through a personal introduction from one of their friends. Brainstorm!

One way to introduce your cause to a group of wealthy people is by asking one supporter to host a little event, such as cocktails, or wine and cheese, where you can present what your group is doing and the forces arrayed against you. Let your host make the decision of whether or not her friends will be comfortable with an overt pitch for donations on the spot.

One of the turning points for the effort to Save South Moresby was when John Broadhead, a key organizer and artist who lived on the Queen Charlotte Islands, came prospecting in Vancouver in the late 1980s. Initially, a high school student asked him to speak at his school. The high school was in the very wealthy community of Shaughnessy, reputed to have more doctors, lawyers, judges, and CEOs per square inch than any other community in Canada. That one talk in the school led to other invitations. He met one sympathetic woman, who agreed to have a small party in her home. She invited a group of friends for Broadhead's slide show. Based on that evening, a core of well-heeled and committed supporters was created. Through the spring and early summer of 1987, nearly sixty thousand dollars was raised to save South Moresby—all stemming from the connections to parents at one high school. Broadhead is a very good fundraiser. His current project, the Gowgaia Institute is doing innovative sustainability projects in Haida Gwaii (the Queen Charlotte Islands). In aid of maintaining the right spiritual attitude to raising funds, his office has a sign: "We are abundant in love and money." A constant panic over scarcity tends to produce scarcity. A loving acceptance of abundance tends to produce abundance.

PREPARING YOUR PITCH

Now that you have gotten your foot in the door to speak to a person of means, you need to prepare. If this person is seriously rich, then people like you (or at least people on the same quest), come to see her fairly regularly. Certain things will be expected before a large cheque is written.

By now you no doubt are expert in presenting your case. You have good visuals of the area you are trying to protect from industrial development. You have clear and well-written fact sheets and can put together an information package that will impress your prospective donor, easy as pie. But for this meeting, you'll need more.

You should prepare a good explanation of your current financial situation, your upcoming expenses, and your likely sources of donations. You will not make a strong impression if all you can offer is that you are up against a huge chemical company, think you may have to go to court, or might have to hold a rally, and need a whole *lot* of money.

Do your homework. It will be well-worthwhile as your group organizes. Your current financial situation is called your financial statement. The upcoming expenses, offset by hoped for donations, is called your budget. Your plan to raise the money is your fundraising plan. If you have someone in your group with a head for numbers, preferably an accountant, ask them for help, especially on the financial statement. Do not write up a budget based only on the money you have in hand. I saw one budget prepared by someone so fiscally conscious that living within one's budget would mandate total inactivity. If the group made a single long-distance phone call, they would be over-budget. Reasonable estimates of money you can raise, but do not yet have in the bank, should be part of your budget.

It is best if you ask to meet with your prospective donor in her home or office. It is a risky proposition to meet for a restaurant meal. As professional fundraiser and advisor to many NGOs, Ken Wyman has pointed out, a restaurant is a terrible place to meet. For one thing, eating and presenting is tricky (spinach in teeth, talking and mumbling, possible Heimlich maneuvers required!). You will also find yourself in an awkward situation at the end of the meal. Who picks up the bill? You asked the prospective donor to lunch, so etiquette says you should pay. But if you pay, you are sending a signal that money is not a problem for your group.

Ask if you can present at their home. This is the most suitable setting as well as being the most convenient place for the possible donor.

When you talk to the prospective donor, he will be able to see your financial needs at a glance. If you need a total of ten thousand dollars, let the donor mull it over. Don't be too precise about what level of financial support you are hoping he can provide. You can make a serious mistake either way. If you say, "We are hoping you can make a donation for ten thousand dollars," the donor may be affronted that you expect her to carry your whole campaign. Worse yet, is asking for a thousand dollars when she'd been contemplating writing a cheque for five thousand. Your most tactful approach is to set out the nature of your situation, the immediacy of your need and say, "We'd be so grateful for anything you can donate toward this challenge. We don't expect that you can make a donation for all of our needs, but any amount will be much appreciated."

Whenever someone does make a donation, large or small, be sure to express your gratitude. Make a point of finding out if your supporter would mind being publicly acknowledged, or if they prefer anonymity. Personalized expressions of gratitude will, of course, mean more than a form letter. You are building a relationship (once again). Find out what drives this donor. What are their personal interests? If they are avid gardeners, a gardening book with the thank you would be appropriate for a large gift. A CD of a favourite singer is a nice way of expressing thanks. Obviously, you do not want to have your thank you suggest you are wasteful with resources. Keep the size of the gift and the personal nature of your thanks in some perspective. If you spot an article in the newspaper on a topic you know is of interest to the donor, clip it and send with a note. You do not want all your contacts with someone, who has been generous, to be about asking for money!

FOUNDATIONS

Charitable foundations exist to support good work done by others. If your group is likely to continue over many years, begins to need money for staff and to execute specific projects, you will quickly find yourself looking for foundation support.

Even though foundations can seem large and impersonal, don't forget that you are still trying to build a relationship. You should remember the names of anyone with whom you speak and you should never send in a proposal without having spoken to someone on the foundation staff.

Many groups make the mistake of writing the perfect proposal. They slave over it for months, crafting it meticulously. It covers all the bases elegantly. It expresses the group's goals, sets out specific project targets and has a well-developed and coherent work-plan and budget. This *magnum opus* is then copied fifty times and mailed all over.

Nothing could be better designed for failure. Never send a proposal that is not tailored to the foundation's own priorities and goals. If your work does not align with the foundation's goals, do not send them a proposal.

Anything you can do to make your proposal stand out is worth trying. One of the early applications for support to save South Moresby was sent in to the foundation in a beautiful Haida bentwood box. Do not be afraid to be beautiful.

It is much easier than it used to be to find out about charitable foundations, their priorities, goals and process. These days, nearly all foundations have a Web site that tells prospective applicants how to proceed. There are often application forms on-line, with critical information about deadlines for grant applications. Some foundations will not accept an unsolicited proposal. Foundations often set out exactly how many pages are acceptable for a letter of inquiry.

Follow the steps set out by the foundation *to the letter.*

Once you are familiar with a foundation's goals, it is a good idea to phone and ask if you can speak with someone about your needs and your project proposal before you send them a full proposal. Foundations often have wonderful people on staff who are happy to review a proposal in draft and give you some helpful hints for improvement. Even if the foundation staff love your proposal, that is not a guarantee the foundation trustees (the ultimate decision-makers) will love it—but it sure doesn't hurt to have someone on the inside rooting for you!

Check the list of trustees. Does anyone in your group have any connection to anyone on the foundation's board? There is no harm in letting any contacts know that you would be very grateful for their support. You can offer to meet with them in advance to help explain your issue and the proposal. If they are not keen, don't push. The foundation staff is there to make sure all the trustees' questions are answered.

Foundations will judge you by your track record. If an interim report is required by a certain date, don't wait for the staff to call and ask for it before you remember it is due! Be professional. Get the work done! And save all your media coverage, plus any letters of support, to send to the foundation with your report.

A good guideline for foundation projects is to "under-promise and over-achieve!"

GOVERNMENT FUNDING

Government funding of environmental groups is much more common in Canada than in the United States. In fact, it is virtually unheard of in the U.S., while, as noted earlier, Canadians often *assume* that environmental groups are funded with tax dollars. There can be programs that meet your needs at the municipal, provincial, and federal levels. You should follow all the same steps that you do for foundations. Check the Web sites for funding programs. Check if your group is eligible. Determine the funding criteria, and tailor your proposal to meet those rules. Contact a real, live person in the branch of government that runs the funding program. Be sure to ask for their advice and make them aware of your work.

Ironically, government funding can be less restrictive than charitable foundation grants. It can often be available to groups that are not registered charities. Government funding can actually make harsher criticism of government possible.

CORPORATE DONATIONS

Asking for money from large corporations can raise ethical concerns. Some organizations, such as Sierra Club of Canada, do not take money from corporations unless they meet a screen for environmental and social impact. Other environmental groups take money from any corporation—even one whose core business is antithetical to the group's goals. Some believe that by engaging with corporations, they can help change them. Others fear that taking corporate money will subtly influence campaigns and blunt effectiveness.

The debate about tainted money is a difficult one. (Although as one wag put it, the problem with tainted money is there "t'ain't enough of it.") You will have to decide for yourselves if taking money from Monsanto or the Shell Environmental Fund is acceptable.

There are many sources of corporate money that are not as close to the bone as money from oil and gas, forestry, or chemical companies. Money from banks, insurance companies and companies with a strong eco-base is accessible through the corporation's publicized philanthropy.

If you decide to pursue money from corporations, the application process is the same as for foundations or governments. Find the rules and then follow them!

LESSONS LEARNED:

1) If you want someone to donate money, you have to ask!
2) Be creative, find ways to raise money in your own community.
3) Always say "please" and make the "thank you" meaningful.

4) Be prepared. Have a sound financial plan.
5) Learn how to budget. Find an accountant. Marry one.
6) Make fundraising *fun*. (It's in there somewhere.)
7) Don't be limited by poverty consciousness. You may not ever have seen a lot of money before, but there is plenty out there.
8) Approach fundraising with the gratitude for gifts about to be received. Be grateful more than needy.
9) Leave no stone unturned.
10) Don't let rejection get to you. It builds character.

Chapter 11

IS IT WORTH IT?

YOU MAY START YOUR LIFE AS AN activist thinking that as soon as you stop that expressway, or save the wetland, or get a municipal bylaw against dangerous pesticides, you will get back to your old life. You may expect that things will get back to normal. In my experience, for most activists, this never happens. Thank God.

The first step of engagement will leave you feeling empowered. Moreover, any notion you may have had that the world runs just fine without your help may be shattered. Suddenly, as if the scales have fallen from your eyes, it becomes increasingly clear that those in power are not very competent. It becomes obvious that you know more about the subject than those who are regulating an industry or making zoning decisions.

Recently I was talking to a construction worker who had become involved in a fight to stop a strip mine near his home. He said, "You know, on a job site, you have to count on everyone. You only hire people who can do their job. They have to be good or they're fired. So I thought it was the same in government. Boy, was I wrong! Those guys couldn't last ten minutes on a job site!"

Once you become aware of the realities of how decisions are made that affect your life, you become politicized. The change in your life can be profound. And it is hard to ever go back to the cocoon-like complacency of those who don't know.

Bobbi Speck, one of the leaders in the 1969 fight to stop the Spadina Expressway (which was to have linked highway 401 to the Gardiner Expressway in Toronto, cutting through and destroying an integrated and intact neighbourhood called "the Annex") wrote about how that successful citizens' campaign changed their lives:

Sometimes the most unlikely people get caught up in events that are bigger than anything they have ever experienced; they find themselves pitted against dark forces they have never dreamed of. Little people become heroes; peaceable folk turn to civil disobedience. Then the historical moment is over for them, and others take up the leadership and the campaign, and the early seminal deeds and the people who did them are forgotten. And life can seemingly return to normal, but the little people are forever changed. This is the theme of *The Hobbit* and the trilogy by J.R.R.Tolkien, and this is something we know in our hearts without being told.[37]

Speck's recollections of the early days, of her waddling to the microphone at her first public hearing, very pregnant and very nervous, will ring chords of memory for many of us. Like Milo, the hero of the children's book *Phantom Tollbooth*, it is just as well you do not know much of the challenges that lie ahead.[38] Milo returned triumphant after a perilous adventure, sent by the Kings Azaz and the Mathemagician to rescue the Princesses Rhyme and Reason from beyond the Mountains of Ignorance. King Azaz reminded him that "there was one very important thing about your quest that we couldn't discuss until you returned."

'I remember,' said Milo eagerly, 'Tell me now.'
'It was impossible,' said the king, looking at the Mathemagician.
'Completely impossible,' said the Mathemagician, looking at the king.
'Do you mean...' stammered the bug who suddenly felt a bit faint.
'Yes, indeed,' they repeated together; 'but if we'd told you then, you might not have gone—and as you've discovered, so many things are possible just as long as you don't know they're impossible.'[39]

Or as Walt Disney once said, "It's kind of fun to do the impossible."

DEUS EX MACHINA

One of the things that inevitably comes to your aid is that which Bobbi Speck identified as synchronicity: "Now there's a phenomenon known as synchronicity. There is, for instance, the example of the monkeys and the fruit: the hundredth monkey phenomenon. You know it: monkeys on different islands—with no contact with each other—simultaneously taking up the practice of washing their fruit. Was this part of the evolution of monkeys? Was it an idea that arrived in common? Synchronicity."[40]

I am not going to attempt an explanation of how and why you should count on synchronicity. This is not a treatise on angels, creative visualization, the power of prayer, the role of miracles, or the actions of chance and random coincidence in our lives. Speck credited "luck and serendipity." No question the frequency of luck increases in direct proportion to your own hard work and passion. Still, I don't have any idea why you can count on amazing strokes of good fortune. I am simply quite certain, based on experience of many campaigns—mine and those of many others—that you can.

In the case of the Spadina Expressway, the campaign was aided by someone no one knew was an ally. Dalton Camp, serving as the Premier Bill Davis's senior advisor at the time, told me the story of how the premier asked him to prepare two different versions of the same speech. In one, Davis was to announce that the Spadina Expressway would proceed. In the other, he would announce it was to be cancelled. When the premier asked for the speeches, Camp told him, "Here's the one where you announce that the expressway is cancelled, and it is such a damn fine speech that I couldn't write the other one."[41]

The expressway was never built, even though initially many community groups had decided the flight was hopeless. The oldest ratepayers group in the city had told the little Annex committee of Speck and her friends that it was too late. Fortunately, they did not accept the "accepted wisdom."

Often activists cannot gauge how much influence they are actually having on decision-makers. It is a common experience to feel frustrated and beleaguered on the verge of total victory. That is why the most essential advice is "Never, give up. Never, ever."

LIFE AS AN ACTIVIST

Life as an activist isn't what anyone would call normal. It is better.

I did not always know this. I remember once when we were in the grip of the herbicide case. My mother had moved in with me at Dalhousie Law School to help out and keep me from following through on my plan to drop out so I would have time for the case. My mother moving in with me kept me in school, but nearly drove me insane. I do not think I have ever had as much stress in my life. My mother felt it too—all the time.

One day she had to spend several hours at a garage to have her car repaired. She was worried about personal money, how the family would get by. (At this point she had sold eighty acres on the Bras d'Or Lakes to pay the bill to Scott Paper.) She was worried about the lawyers' bills, my school work, the threat that the spraying with Agent Orange would take place if we lost the case. The mechanic began to talk to her about the herbicide issue. He'd seen it on the news. She was astonished by what he had said, "I really envy you. I go to work every day. I fix cars. I never know if my life really means anything. You know. Your life really makes a difference."

She went from feeling sorry for herself, to feeling lucky. So did I.

Most of the experience of activism is positive. Sure it adds a different sort of pressure to your life, but it gives you far more. You make friends you would never have known otherwise. You can meet people you always admired from afar. In 1975, I would never have imagined I would ever meet Dr. David Suzuki, Maude Barlow, or Farley Mowat. Now, they are among my best friends. In grade ten I was influenced to become an environmentalist by the writings of David Brower. I never would have imagined getting to know him, but I did. I even drank one of his fabulous martinis. (He travelled with a clean Hellman's mayo jar, gin, and vermouth. It was so thrilling to realize my hero could mix a good martini.)

The marvelous truth about the environmental movement is that there is no hierarchy. We are all in this together.

Marshall McLuhan's "global village" was a place where he thought we would "re-tribalize" ourselves.

This is what I think we are doing in the environmental movement. We are re-tribalizing ourselves. Some have commented on the tribal aspects of clothing and culture. Some may want to belong to "Clan Gap" or parade as members of the cult known as "Tommy Hilfiger."

There are other ways to create new tribes with meaning. The movement is my extended family. I think nothing (but gratitude) of asking for a place to sleep in homes across Canada. When my daughter was small, I always asked for a place to stay where someone had children about her age. So, she has grown up knowing kids across the country. I can close my eyes and picture the bed I sleep in whether in Victoria, or Saskatoon, Halifax, or Calgary. I travel a lot, but do not suffer from that *Lost in Translation*-feeling of the eternal sameness of hotel life. I am always home.

Reciprocity in building "billeting karma" also matters, and my house is home to just about any and all weary environmental travellers. (Only those with severe pet allergies have given my place a miss.) We have met so many wonderful people through sharing space and meals and wine.

The people you meet will increasingly be people who share your values.

The movement of like-minded souls, whether in the environmental, human-rights, or development movements, is its own kind of community. It may be a true local community. It may be a global community, linked through e-mails and phone calls. A community based on shared values and ideals is a wonderful place to live.

There is a lot of discussion these days about work-life balance. This may well be important if working in a corporate culture. However, I do not think it fits in thinking about our work in the environmental movement. Saving the world is not a nine-to-five commitment. Environmentally aware people do not stop recycling because they are on vacation. I don't stop letting people know about why the weather is so unpredictable because I was not asked to give a lecture to a climate change conference. A cab driver in Washington, D.C. is just as important to educate as a science teacher in Alberta.

This life is not work. This life is a life.

The experience of campaigning, of moving from hobbit to hero status as Bobbi Speck put it, will give you far more than you can imagine at the outset. No day will ever be just like the day before or the day after. Amazing events will happen to you and around you.

Here are some of my favourite, cherished memories, made all the more precious by the complete incongruity of the experience:

- Dancing in the sand with Bella Abzug at a beach in Miami while Leslie Gore sang, "It's My Party" for the World Women's Congress delegates.

- Drinking caipirinhas under the stars in a small Amazonian village with *seringueiro* activists (rubber-tappers who work to protect the rainforest).
- Dancing with an exuberant crowd of Earth Charter activists to the music of Mali singer Oumou Sangare in the Royal Tropical Museum of The Netherlands, with even Her Majesty Queen Beatrix, joining in (and making her security guards rather nervous).[42]
- Watching Sir Peter Ustinov become Hercule Poirot for a small audience of me and my daughter in the break of a World Federalist conference in London.
- Talking about her kids' activities in the church choir, while having dinner at the Nairobi home of Wangari Matthai, founder of the Greenbelt Movement, and a future Nobel Peace Prize recipient.
- Singing Christmas carols at the home of the highest ranking U.S. diplomat in Cuba with the tree adorned with Uncle Sam Santa Clauses, and rifle-toting Marines outside. (I never had realized so many far-right Republicans were operating in Havanna.)
- Being defended by members of the band The Turtles when they were, like me, on Peter Gowski's television show, *Ninety Minutes Live* under the group's new name Flo and Eddie. Journalist and future MP, John Harvard, had been giving me a hard time for being originally from the U.S. ("We're from the U.S. and you pay us!" the band had interjected.)
- Listening to Mikhail Gorbachev expound on Jesus' Sermon on the Mount as the inspiration for the Earth Charter, which we were drafting in a small hotel conference room in Rio.
- Hearing the Dalai Lama tell, amid much laughter (his own), about how the security guards at the Vancouver airport had seized the small knife he carried to peel fruit.

None of these moments could possibly have happened in a normal life.

I could have had a normal life. I could have had a normal legal career. I'd be a partner in some big firm by now. I'd be making tons of money. I make less now than the secretary at my old law firm.

Money is a poor substitute for having an interesting life.

NEVER GIVE UP AND NEVER STOP LAUGHING

At a recent activist training session in Charlottetown, Prince Edward Island, a woman fighting a solid waste dump in her neighbourhood told about a slew of events that would make Pollyanna weep: winning court cases; quashing a permit but having the permit re-issued; legal bills piling up; a snare of procedural wrangling that left me dizzy just hearing about it. She laughed, "At every meeting, we just keep saying, 'This will be a movie!' It's too bizarre not to be. So we are all deciding who we want to play us!" (She had dibs on Meryl Streep.)

Next to passion and tenacity, your sense of humour is your most important asset. In fact, it is hard to know how you will be able to hold on to tenacity and passion without a good laugh now and then.

At the worst moments in the herbicide case, when we were being threatened with poison and financial ruin, my brother would say to me, a maniacal grin on his face, "We've got the bastards on the run now!" It never failed to make me laugh. Sometimes gallows humour is all you have.

Laughter helps propel the political insights of the Raging Grannies and the Radical Cheerleaders. Political satire and ridicule are the very best ways to deflate a tyrant. Recall the last moments of the Nicolae Ceauflescu regime in Romania. He had organized a rally, hand-picked and bussed-in supporters. His speech from the balcony was televised live nationally. He was an iron-fisted and unstoppable leader, until the television cameras caught his reaction to a handful of students in the crowd. They were heckling him. They were jeering. He suddenly looked frightened and unsure of himself. The curtain was pulled back on the Great and Powerful Wizard and the whole country could see the small and timid man at the controls. People laughed. He was deposed within days.

The pen is mightier than the sword. Laughter may be more fatal.[43]

For you own health and sanity, humour is essential. Norman Cousins credited laughter with boosting his immune system and saving his life. "Laughter is internal jogging," he wrote.[44]

A sense of humour is indispensable.

JOIN US

Our goal is always to involve more and more people in the business of protecting life on Earth. We are like a big, noisy, fun, street parade. The circus come to town. At first we can just see a few people peeking out from behind the curtains. Gradually, the less timid come out of their homes. With time, they line the streets cheering us on. We will not have won until the vast crowd stops observing, steps down from the curb and joins the march.

That progression from observer to participant is the key moment in turning an average person into a superhero.

Step off the curb and join us.

Yes, saving the world in your spare time may involve sacrifices. You may (will) have less money. You may spend too many nights and weekends in meetings. However, on balance, you will get far more than you give. I promise.

A life that is meaningful, every single day, is rare in this world.

Your life was a gift to you. Make it a gift to the world.

Appendix A
MY FAVOURITE QUOTES

"When we try to pick out anything by itself, we find it hitched to everything else in the universe."—John Muir, Sierra Club founder

"If we don't change our course, we'll wind up where we are headed."
—Chinese proverb

"Never doubt that a small group of thoughtful, committed people can change the world. Indeed, it is the only thing that ever has."—Margaret Mead speaking at the parallel NGO event at the 1972 Stockholm UN Conference on the Human Environment

"Why is it whenever we destroy something man made, it's called vandalism? And whenever we destroy something God made, it's called progress?"
—former Democratic senator of Arkansas, Dale Bumpers

"Our lives begin to end the day we become silent about things that matter."—Dr.Martin Luther King, Jr.

"The world shrinks or expands in proportion to one's courage."
—Anais Nin

"In wildness is the preservation of the world."—Henry David Thoreau

"Ever since Adam ate the apple, man has refrained from no folly of which he was capable. The End."—Bertrand Russell *History of the World for Martian Infant Schools*, a one-page manuscript written by Lord Russell, who gave it to my mother

"We have met the enemy and he is us."—Walt Kelly, creator of *Pogo*

"Truth is stranger than fiction, because fiction is obliged to stick to the possibilities."—Mark Twain

"Earth provides enough to satisfy every man's need, but not every man's greed."—Gandhi

"Sustainable Development: development that meets the needs of the present generation without sacrificing the ability of future generations to meet their needs."—World Commission on Environment and Development

"We travel together, passengers on a little spaceship, dependent on its vulnerable resources of air and soil; all committed for our safety to its security and peace; preserved from annihilation only by the care, the work, and, I will say, the love we give our fragile craft."—Adlai Stevenson from his last speech as U.S. ambassador to the United Nations

"Humanity is conducting an unintended, uncontrolled, globally pervasive experiment whose ultimate consequences are second only to global nuclear war."—Consensus Statement from "Our Changing Atmosphere: Implications for Global Security," the First International Scientific Conference on Climate Change, Toronto, Ontario, June 1988

"Every time history repeats itself, the price goes up."—Ronald Wright's citation of graffiti in *A Short History of Progress*

"No more TV until you clean up your planet."—1990s-era Sierra Club T-shirt

"Nature bats last."—1970s-era bumper sticker

"Any environmental group with money in the bank simply doesn't understand the severity of the problem."—David Brower

"The environmental movement is the only one that circles the wagons and shoots inward."—David Brower

MEDIA MATERIALS

NOTICE TO MEDIA:

PRESS CONFERENCE
"THE REAL COST OF NUCLEAR ENERGY"—Citizens for Sane Energy Choices will reveal the results of a complete analysis of the economic burden of nuclear power.

DATE: TUESDAY, SEPTEMBER XX, 200X
TIME: 10:30 A.M.
LOCATION: Your best local place

Speakers: Dr. J.K. Galbraith
            Prof. Amory Torrie
Contact: Joe Media-guy at (613) 241-4611 for advance interviews or embargoed copies of the report.

(In areas where bilingual media is expected, issue a translation at the same time in French or Spanish as appropriate.)

DRAFT PRESS RELEASE:

[Headline: try for short and sexy]
DESTROYING WETLANDS WILL INCREASE COSTS TO TAXPAYERS
For Immediate Release [or state date and time on which release can be public and write]
EMBARGOED FOR RELEASE UNTIL [set date and time]

[Text: keep to the five W's (who, what, where, when, why). The first sentence should set the context. Stay clear, factual, and concise.]

[Always state the place from which release originates at top of first paragraph]

(Ottawa): Citizens Organized to Protect Wetlands today announced the results of its audit of the costs of the proposed Department of Boondoggles development in the Amphibia Wetlands.

[intersperse with quotes.]

"By our calculations, reviewed by the firm of Somebody Credible Ltd., the Department of Boondoggles will be increasing the provincial deficit by $300 million by choosing this environmentally sensitive site, instead of merely revamping their existing building," said group chair, J.Q. Public.

Citizens Organized to Protect Wetlands is considering legal action if its current petition campaign is unsuccessful in persuading the Minister of Boondoggles to reconsider. A demonstration is also planned in front of the Department's headquarters, to take place next Wednesday, the XXth of XX, at 12 noon.

"We are confident that good sense will prevail" said group researcher I.M. Green, "With the provincial election in the offing, and so many environmentally concerned statements coming form the Premier's office, we simply cannot believe that this deliberately wrong-headed policy will prevail."

[It is a convention of news releases that they end with a –30–. It tells reporters that the text has ended.]

–30–
Contact:
I. M. Green: 503-555-1111
J.Q. Public: 503-626-1212

[Reminder: make sure your contacts are available to media on this day at those numbers!]

KEYS TO EFFECTIVE LETTER-WRITING

To the editor:
1) Be brief (two hundred to three hundred words).
2) Be relevant. (Cite a story in the same newspaper and comment on it.)
3) If possible, be ironic. Be witty. Pack a punch.
4) Always include all the information required by that newspaper. Check the letters page to be sure.

To politicians:
1) Length does not matter, but effective letters state your position in the first line!
2) Include a specific request or question that requires a specific answer. This may defeat the form-letter reply. If you receive a form letter that is not responsive to your question, write again!
3) Be respectful, but be clear.
4) Sign your letter, include contact information.

Appendix C

THE EARTH CHARTER

PREAMBLE

We stand at a critical moment in Earth's history, a time when humanity must choose its future. As the world becomes increasingly interdependent and fragile, the future at once holds great peril and great promise. To move forward we must recognize that in the midst of a magnificent diversity of cultures and life forms we are one human family and one Earth community with a common destiny. We must join together to bring forth a sustainable global society founded on respect for nature, universal human rights, economic justice, and a culture of peace. Towards this end, it is imperative that we, the peoples of Earth, declare our responsibility to one another, to the greater community of life, and to future generations.

EARTH, OUR HOME

Humanity is part of a vast evolving universe. Earth, our home, is alive with a unique community of life. The forces of nature make existence a demanding and uncertain adventure, but Earth has provided the conditions essential to life's evolution. The resilience of the community of life and the well-being of humanity depend upon preserving a healthy biosphere with all its ecological systems, a rich variety of plants and animals, fertile soils, pure waters, and clean air. The global environment with its finite resources is a common concern of all peoples. The protection of Earth's vitality, diversity, and beauty is a sacred trust.

THE GLOBAL SITUATION

The dominant patterns of production and consumption are causing environmental devastation, the depletion of resources, and a massive extinction of species. Communities are being undermined. The benefits of development are not shared equitably and the gap between rich and poor is widening. Injustice, poverty, ignorance, and violent conflict are widespread and the cause of great suffering. An unprecedented rise in human population has overburdened ecological and social systems. The foundations of global security are threatened. These trends are perilous—but not inevitable.

THE CHALLENGES AHEAD

The choice is ours: form a global partnership to care for Earth and one another or risk the destruction of ourselves and the diversity of life. Fundamental changes are needed in our values, institutions, and ways of living. We must realize that when basic needs have been met, human development is primarily about being more, not having more. We have the knowledge and technology to provide for all and to reduce our impacts on the environment. The emergence of a global civil society is creating new opportunities to build a democratic and humane world. Our environmental, economic, political, social, and spiritual challenges are interconnected, and together we can forge inclusive solutions.

UNIVERSAL RESPONSIBILITY

To realize these aspirations, we must decide to live with a sense of universal responsibility, identifying ourselves with the whole Earth community as well as our local communities. We are at once citizens of different nations and of one world in which the local and global are linked. Everyone shares responsibility for the present and future well-being of the human family and the larger living world. The spirit of human solidarity and kinship with all life is strengthened when we live with reverence for the mystery of being, gratitude for the gift of life, and humility regarding the human place in nature.

We urgently need a shared vision of basic values to provide an ethical foundation for the emerging world community. Therefore, together in hope we affirm the following interdependent principles for a sustainable way of life as a common standard by which the conduct of all individuals, organizations, businesses, governments, and transnational institutions is to be guided and assessed.

PRINCIPLES

I. RESPECT AND CARE FOR THE COMMUNITY OF LIFE

1. Respect Earth and life in all its diversity.
   a. Recognize that all beings are interdependent and every form of life has value regardless of its worth to human beings.
   b. Affirm faith in the inherent dignity of all human beings and in the intellectual, artistic, ethical, and spiritual potential of humanity.
2. Care for the community of life with understanding, compassion, and love.
   a. Accept that with the right to own, manage, and use natural resources comes the duty to prevent environmental harm and to protect the rights of people.
   b. Affirm that with increased freedom, knowledge, and power comes increased responsibility to promote the common good.
3. Build democratic societies that are just, participatory, sustainable, and peaceful.
   a. Ensure that communities at all levels guarantee human rights and fundamental freedoms and provide everyone an opportunity to realize his or her full potential.
   b. Promote social and economic justice, enabling all to achieve a secure and meaningful livelihood that is ecologically responsible.
4. Secure Earth's bounty and beauty for present and future generations.
   a. Recognize that the freedom of action of each generation is qualified by the needs of future generations.
   b. Transmit to future generations values, traditions, and institutions that support the long-term flourishing of Earth's human and ecological communities.

In order to fulfill these four broad commitments, it is necessary to:

II. ECOLOGICAL INTEGRITY

5. Protect and restore the integrity of Earth's ecological systems, with special concern for biological diversity and the natural processes that sustain life.

   a. Adopt at all levels sustainable development plans and regulations that make environmental conservation and rehabilitation integral to all development initiatives.

   b. Establish and safeguard viable nature and biosphere reserves, including wild lands and marine areas, to protect Earth's life-support systems, maintain biodiversity, and preserve our natural heritage.

   c. Promote the recovery of endangered species and ecosystems.

   d. Control and eradicate non-native or genetically modified organisms harmful to native species and the environment, and prevent introduction of such harmful organisms.

   e. Manage the use of renewable resources such as water, soil, forest products, and marine life in ways that do not exceed rates of regeneration and that protect the health of ecosystems.

   f. Manage the extraction and use of non-renewable resources such as minerals and fossil fuels in ways that minimize depletion and cause no serious environmental damage.

6. Prevent harm as the best method of environmental protection and, when knowledge is limited, apply a precautionary approach.

   a. Take action to avoid the possibility of serious or irreversible environmental harm even when scientific knowledge is incomplete or inconclusive.

   b. Place the burden of proof on those who argue that a proposed activity will not cause significant harm, and make the responsible parties liable for environmental harm.

   c. Ensure that decision-making addresses the cumulative, long-term, indirect, long-distance, and global consequences of human activities.

   d. Prevent pollution of any part of the environment and allow no build-up of radioactive, toxic, or other hazardous substances.

   e. Avoid military activities damaging to the environment.

7. Adopt patterns of production, consumption, and reproduction that safeguard Earth's regenerative capacities, human rights, and community well-being.

   a. Reduce, reuse, and recycle the materials used in production and consumption systems, and ensure that residual waste can be assimilated by ecological systems.

   b. Act with restraint and efficiency when using energy, and rely increasingly on renewable energy sources such as solar and wind.

   c. Promote the development, adoption, and equitable transfer of environmentally sound technologies.

   d. Internalize the full environmental and social costs of goods and services in the selling price, and enable consumers to identify products that meet the highest social and environmental standards.

   e. Ensure universal access to health care that fosters reproductive health and responsible reproduction.

   f. Adopt lifestyles that emphasize the quality of life and material sufficiency in a finite world.

8. Advance the study of ecological sustainability and promote the open exchange and wide application of the knowledge acquired.

   a. Support international scientific and technical cooperation on sustainability, with special attention to the needs of developing nations.

   b. Recognize and preserve the traditional knowledge and spiritual wisdom in all cultures that contribute to environmental protection and human well-being.

   c. Ensure that information of vital importance to human health and environmental protection, including genetic information, remains available in the public domain.

III. SOCIAL AND ECONOMIC JUSTICE

9. Eradicate poverty as an ethical, social, and environmental imperative.

    a. Guarantee the right to potable water, clean air, food security, uncontaminated soil, shelter, and safe sanitation, allocating the national and international resources required.

    b. Empower every human being with the education and resources to secure a sustainable livelihood, and provide social security and safety nets for those who are unable to support themselves.

    c. Recognize the ignored, protect the vulnerable, serve those who suffer, and enable them to develop their capacities and to pursue their aspirations.

10. Ensure that economic activities and institutions at all levels promote human development in an equitable and sustainable manner.

    a. Promote the equitable distribution of wealth within nations and among nations.

    b. Enhance the intellectual, financial, technical, and social resources of developing nations, and relieve them of onerous international debt.

    c. Ensure that all trade supports sustainable resource use, environmental protection, and progressive labor standards.

    d. Require multinational corporations and international financial organizations to act transparently in the public good, and hold them accountable for the consequences of their activities.

11. Affirm gender equality and equity as prerequisites to sustainable development and ensure universal access to education, health care, and economic opportunity.

    a. Secure the human rights of women and girls and end all violence against them.

    b. Promote the active participation of women in all aspects of economic, political, civil, social, and cultural life as full and equal partners, decision-makers, leaders, and beneficiaries.

    c. Strengthen families and ensure the safety and loving nurture of all family members.

12. Uphold the right of all, without discrimination, to a natural and social environment supportive of human dignity, bodily health, and spiritual well-being, with special attention to the rights of indigenous peoples and minorities.

a. Eliminate discrimination in all its forms, such as that based on race, color, sex, sexual orientation, religion, language, and national, ethnic or social origin.

b. Affirm the right of indigenous peoples to their spirituality, knowledge, lands and resources and to their related practice of sustainable livelihoods.

c. Honor and support the young people of our communities, enabling them to fulfill their essential role in creating sustainable societies.

d. Protect and restore outstanding places of cultural and spiritual significance.

IV. DEMOCRACY, NONVIOLENCE, AND PEACE

13. Strengthen democratic institutions at all levels, and provide transparency and accountability in governance, inclusive participation in decision-making, and access to justice.

a. Uphold the right of everyone to receive clear and timely information on environmental matters and all development plans and activities which are likely to affect them or in which they have an interest

b. Support local, regional and global civil society, and promote the meaningful participation of all interested individuals and organizations in decision-making.

c. Protect the rights to freedom of opinion, expression, peaceful assembly, association, and dissent.

d. Institute effective and efficient access to administrative and independent judicial procedures, including remedies and redress for environmental harm and the threat of such harm.

e. Eliminate corruption in all public and private institutions.

f. Strengthen local communities, enabling them to care for their environments, and assign environmental responsibilities to the levels of government where they can be carried out most effectively.

14. Integrate into formal education and lifelong learning the knowledge, values, and skills needed for a sustainable way of life.

    a. Provide all, especially children and youth, with educational opportunities that empower them to contribute actively to sustainable development.

    b. Promote the contribution of the arts and humanities as well as the sciences in sustainability education.

    c. Enhance the role of the mass media in raising awareness of ecological and social challenges.

    d. Recognize the importance of moral and spiritual education for sustainable living.

15. Treat all living beings with respect and consideration.

    a. Prevent cruelty to animals kept in human societies and protect them from suffering.

    b. Protect wild animals from methods of hunting, trapping, and fishing that cause extreme, prolonged, or avoidable suffering.

    c. Avoid or eliminate to the fullest extent possible the taking or destruction of non-targeted species.

16. Promote a culture of tolerance, nonviolence, and peace.

    a. Encourage and support mutual understanding, solidarity, and cooperation among all peoples and within and among nations.

    b. Implement comprehensive strategies to prevent violent conflict and use collaborative problem solving to manage and resolve environmental conflicts and other disputes.

    d. Demilitarize national security systems to the level of a non-provocative defense posture, and convert military resources to peaceful purposes, including ecological restoration.

    e. Eliminate nuclear, biological, and toxic weapons and other weapons of mass destruction.

    f. Ensure that the use of orbital and outer space supports environmental protection and peace.

    g. Recognize that peace is the wholeness created by right relationships with oneself, other persons, other cultures, other life, Earth, and the larger whole of which all are a part.

THE WAY FORWARD

As never before in history, common destiny beckons us to seek a new beginning. Such renewal is the promise of these Earth Charter principles.

To fulfill this promise, we must commit ourselves to adopt and promote the values and objectives of the Charter.

This requires a change of mind and heart. It requires a new sense of global interdependence and universal responsibility. We must imaginatively develop and apply the vision of a sustainable way of life locally, nationally, regionally, and globally. Our cultural diversity is a precious heritage and different cultures will find their own distinctive ways to realize the vision. We must deepen and expand the global dialogue that generated the Earth Charter, for we have much to learn from the ongoing collaborative search for truth and wisdom.

Life often involves tensions between important values. This can mean difficult choices. However, we must find ways to harmonize diversity with unity, the exercise of freedom with the common good, short-term objectives with long-term goals. Every individual, family, organization, and community has a vital role to play. The arts, sciences, religions, educational institutions, media, businesses, nongovernmental organizations, and governments are all called to offer creative leadership. The partnership of government, civil society, and business is essential for effective governance.

In order to build a sustainable global community, the nations of the world must renew their commitment to the United Nations, fulfill their obligations under existing international agreements, and support the implementation of Earth Charter principles with an international legally binding instrument on environment and development.

Let ours be a time remembered for the awakening of a new reverence for life, the firm resolve to achieve sustainability, the quickening of the struggle for justice and peace, and the joyful celebration of life.

Appendix D

A USER'S GUIDE TO FREEDOM OF INFORMATION LEGISLATION
BY KEN RUBIN

CITIZEN ACTIVISTS ARE ON THE FRONT lines on many current issues. But they are usually well back in line in utilizing and accessing government records where actions are discussed and strategies adopted that affect them.

Finding out information about contaminated sites, poor airline safety, lobbying going on for government contracts, and more requires an information battle plan.

So where to begin if you've never tried to pry government records from their protective nests?

Before trying the formal access process, it's a good idea to search out and call the relevant agency to see what information there is available without having to go through the access rules. Some jurisdictions also produce a registry index of the type of records available from their agencies.

If the only route to get the data is access legislation, then ascertain whether the data sought is held by an agency covered by the legislation. For instance, not all provincial-territorial acts cover local municipalities or special bodies like hospitals, universities and government-funded social service agencies. Or venture into using corporate disclosure codes.

To make an access application, it is crucial to be as specific as possible. That can include specifying dates, the type of records sought, and a limited subject matter. Remember that the request is not in the form of questions, but for the provision of records.

It doesn't hurt to state that you are willing to discuss with authorities what you are seeking.

Most jurisdictions want you to put the request to a specific agency with the applicable application fee. Some jurisdictions want the applicant to use forms.

Once you have ended up framing and filing an access application, bear in mind the following factors:

- This is not an instant disclosure process.
- Records do not have to be released for at least thirty days, with the likelihood that time can extended if there is third party data involved or legitimate consultations required.

It's an information-seeking procedure fraught with many legal exceptions to disclosure. Those exemptions can vary in different jurisdictions.

Exemption claims range from commercial confidentiality, policy advice, lawyer-client privilege in relation to law enforcement matters. Some matters, like cabinet confidences, are either totally excluded or exempted from release for many years. Some exemptions are mandatory; others discretionary.

Unfortunately, in most access legislation, there is a limited public health, safety and environment, public interest provision that only occasionally overrides some of the exemptions cited. Not all agencies or branches within an agency interpret exemptions the very same way, that is, when they do supply records and when they record their actions.

Fees can be assessed for manual or computer search for, and preparation of records, for computer programming, and copying. This can add up. It's best to get an explanation when fees are assessed. Records—like e-mails—can, for instance, be key records of behind-the-scenes happenings. But they can generate large fee estimates. Narrowing an application can, at times, reduce fee estimates as can viewing records in person.

It's in your interest to keep track of progress on requests made through calls and a written log. If there are delays or excessive fees, these are matters you have a right to complain about to an information commissioner or ombudsman in most jurisdictions.

Do not expect a proactive access service. Only some jurisdictions have designated access officers available. Remember, the art of negotiation is continually part of the process.

Once records (if any) are received, the data should be checked to see if that's what you wanted. Sometimes, a response comes in bits and pieces through more than one reply. Your appeal rights include complaining about exemptions and incomplete responses. Complaints usually have to made within a specified time period from thirty days to one year. Further review upon information commissioner findings can be made to the courts.

Getting records does not end your work. Using the information received or publicizing the lack of sufficient response are part of an access strategy. You may be able to seek help from your political representatives or various public interest groups and advocates.

What access can help do is create more transparency for everyone and every group. It would be of great assistance too if access laws were radically improved. I, for one, advocate this and have developed a Public Right to Know Act for discussion and action.

I've worked with many individuals and groups seeking information. It's not an easy answer-all process, say, when you are trying to get drug safety data. But it can make the difference and cannot be ignored or left to experts or to those who want more secrecy and fewer improvements.

To recap, here are the steps in making an access to information request:

- Identify the target department and ensure that it is the correct one. For example, is Health Canada the agency responsible for developing Canada's Food Guide?
- Ask for specific records related to a specific time period. What submissions were made concerning Canada's Food Guide? Were internal studies conducted? Focus groups? What costs were involved?
- File your request (this costs five dollars federally in Canada), and indicate you want to be contacted when the request is received.
- Be persistent and monitor progress. Has the agency gone to the appropriate branches? What's delaying the response? Why are fees so high?
- Keep a log of the service you receive.
- Check what been received. Why is the correspondence from the food industry missing? The exemptions that prevented the release of documents on policy advice or commercial confidentiality need an explanation.

- Review whether you need to appeal. If crucial data are withheld, seek help from the Information Commissioner.
- Don't stop there. Ask for further details, and then publicize the information you have received—or the failure of the agency to provide it.
- Remember, what it takes to engage in access is curiosity with a good dose of persistence.
- Keep fine tuning your information-seeking skills and don't stop going after essential data you need.

Ken Rubin is a long-time, Ottawa-based, public interest researcher who has used the access process many times. He has a special interest in health, safety, environmental, consumer, and civil liberty issues.

Appendix E

PETITIONING THE HOUSE OF COMMONS
A PRACTICAL GUIDE

I. DRAFTING A PETITION

A petition cannot be presented to the House of Commons unless it has first been submitted by a Member of Parliament to the Clerk of Petitions for certification. In order to be certified, the petition must meet certain requirements established by the rules and practices of the House. The following list sets out guidelines for drafting petitions on matters of public concern.

General requirements

- The petition must be handwritten, typed, printed or photocopied on sheets of paper of usual size, i.e. measuring 21.5 cm × 28 cm (8½ × 11 inches) or 21.5 cm × 35.5 cm (8½ × 14 inches).
- The words "To the House of Commons" or "To the House of Commons in Parliament assembled" must appear at the beginning of the petition. Petitions to the Government of Canada, the Prime Minister, a Minister, or an individual Member of Parliament are not acceptable.
- The petition must be respectful and use temperate language.
- The text of the petition must not be altered either by erasing or crossing out words or by adding words.
- No other matter is to be attached or appended to or written on the petition, whether in the form of additional documents, maps, pictures, news articles, explanatory or supporting statements, or requests for support. A return address is allowed.
- The petition must concern a subject within the authority of the Parliament of Canada. The petition must not concern a purely provincial or municipal matter or any matter which should be brought before a court of law or a tribunal.

Prayer

- The petition must contain a request, called a "prayer," for Parliament to take some action (or refrain from taking some action) to remedy a grievance. A statement of grievance or a statement of opinion alone cannot be received as a petition. The petition must not, however, *demand* or *insist* that Parliament do something.
- The "prayer" should be clear and to the point. Details which the petitioners think important may be included in the statement of grievance.

Signatures and addresses

- Some signatures and addresses should, if possible, appear on the first sheet with the "prayer". The subject-matter of the petition must be indicated on each of the other sheets containing signatures and addresses.
- The petition must contain a *minimum* of 25 valid signatures, each with the address of the petitioner. The signature of a Member of Parliament is not counted.
- Each petitioner must sign his or her own name directly on the petition and must not sign for anyone else. Names should be signed, not printed. Signatures cannot be attached to a sheet (taped or pasted on) or photocopied onto it. If a petitioner cannot sign because of illness or a disability, this must be noted on the petition and the note signed by a witness.
- The petitioner's address must be written directly on the petition and not pasted on or reproduced. The petitioner may give his or her full home address or simply the city and province.
- Aliens not resident in Canada cannot petition the House of Commons of Canada.

Form of a petition

- The recommended form of a petition to the House of Commons is set out on the last page of this guide. Below is a ficticious model petition.

PETITION

TO THE HOUSE OF COMMONS IN PARLIAMENT ASSEMBLED

- We, the undersigned residents of Canada, draw the attention of the House to the following:
- THAT incidents of X are becoming more and more frequent;
- THAT each incident of X harms the public; and
- THAT there would be fewer such incidents if certain legislative measures were taken
- THEREFORE, your petitioners call upon Parliament to enact legislation against X.

- On the other sheets of signatures and addresses, the subject-matter of this fictitious petition could be shown as follows: *PETITION ASKING PARLIAMENT TO ENACT LEGISLATION AGAINST X.*

II. SUBMITTING A PETITION TO THE HOUSE

- Only a Member of Parliament can present a petition to the House of Commons. The petitioners must send their petition to a Member with a request to present it to the House. Any Member of Parliament may be asked to present the petition even if he or she does not represent the petitioners.
- Nothing in the rules or practices of the House of Commons requires a Member to present a petition he or she has received. The Member may even ask another Member to present the petition.
- Members of the public who wish to petition the House of Commons on a matter of public interest are advised to first submit a draft petition (without signatures) to a Member of Parliament to see whether it is correctly worded and whether the Member would agree to present it.
- A Member may present a petition to the House in either of two ways: by making a brief statement in the House regarding the origin and subject of the petition, or by filing the petition with the Clerk of the House while the House is sitting. The act of presenting a petition does not necessarily mean that the Member supports it.

- If a Member makes a statement in the House when presenting a petition, the statement is reproduced in *Hansard*, the official record of the debates. A record of each petition presented, whether or not a statement is made, appears in the *Journals* for that day.
- Once the petition has been presented, it is sent to the Government, which must table a response in the House within 45 days.

Clerk of Petitions
Private Members' Business Office
Room 131-N
Centre Block
House of Commons
Tel (613) 992-9511
Fax (613) 947-7626

FORM OF A PETITION

The recommended form of a petition to the House of Commons is set out below.

PETITION
TO THE HOUSE OF COMMONS
IN PARLIAMENT ASSEMBLED

We, the undersigned   *Here identify, in general terms, who the petitioners are, for example:*
- *citizens (or residents) of Canada*
- *electors of (name of electoral district)*
- *residents of the Province of....*
- *residents of the City (or Village or Township, etc.) of....*

draw the attention of the House to the following:

THAT   *Here briefly state the reasons underlying the request for the intervention of the House by outlining the grievance or problem or by sum-marizing the facts which the petitioners wish the House to consider.*

| THEREFORE, your petitioners | Request that Parliament *or* call upon Parliament to | *Here set out the "prayer" or request by stating succinctly what action the petitioners wish Parliament to take or what action it should refrain from taking.* |

	Signatures (Sign your own name. Do not print)		Addresses (Give your full home address or your city and province)

THEREFORE, your petitioners   *Here repeat the "prayer" from the first page of the petition.*

	Signatures (Sign your own name. Do not print)		Addresses (Give your full home address or your city and province)

Petition concerning   *Here state the subject matter of the petition.*

	Signatures (Sign your own name. Do not print)		Addresses (Give your full home address or your city and province)

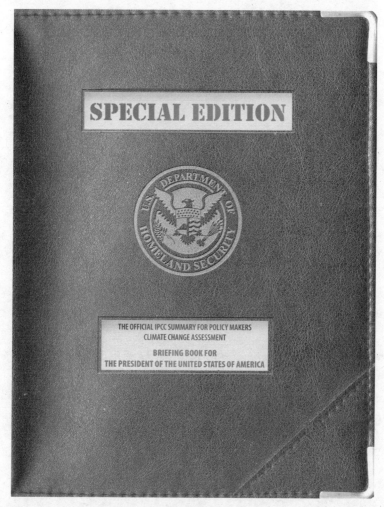

SPECIAL EDITION

U.S. DEPARTMENT OF HOMELAND SECURITY

THE OFFICIAL IPCC SUMMARY FOR POLICY MAKERS
CLIMATE CHANGE ASSESSMENT

BRIEFING BOOK FOR
THE PRESIDENT OF THE UNITED STATES OF AMERICA

life on earth is possible because it is not too hot and not too cold! It is kept JUST RIGHT by something called a carbon cycle.

OXYGEN

CO²

life is also possible because there is air to breathe. For both of these things we should thank God and the plants and the carbon cycle.

Carbon dioxide is sucked in by plants and the plants give us oxygen!

George, did you ever wonder where the oil, coal and gas came from? It was from those trees stomped down by the dinosaurs!

That's why they are called "fossil fuels" and they are full of all that carbon stored up by the trees a very long time ago...even before there were people on the Earth.

(note to George: the seven days in Genesis is not a real time line. There were not people on the earth at the same time as the dinosaurs.)

Humans are very clever!

We figured out how to get energy from the old trees. When we burned up those old trees, all that carbon from millions of years of the sun's energy got released fast!

The problem is that we put out so much carbon, so fast, that all our friends, the green leafy things, and the oceans and all the places carbon went to keep things in balance could not keep up.

Carbon is out of balance!

What happens when the carbon is out of whack? Lots of bad things happen.

BIG storms, more droughts! More forest fires! More floods. A melting Arctic and no polar bears!

(note to George: We know you do not worry much about stuff like this because you have lots and lots of money. And you don't much care about polar bears and it will be cool when there's no ice at the North Pole and you can drive big boats right over the top of the world to make more money. And it is true you and your friends can likely get somewhere safe and leave those people who aren't worth saving anyway behind because you figure if God loved them they'd have their own SUV by now. And if they are lucky they get to go into one of those cool stadiums where nice people bring them stuff....but there are storms coming so big, even you cannot get away from them....)

It is people all around the world telling you to stop being a bad, bad boy.

Stop being selfish!

Start sharing all your toys and stop spoiling it for everyone else.

Tell all your friends, all the nice people at Exxon and Chevron, that the party's over.

No more fossil fuels to waste.
No more time to waste.

(Note to George: There is some really good stuff to read on this at Matthew chapters 5-7. It is called the "Sermon on the Mount." You should read it. Soon.)

The End

NOTES

CHAPTER 1

1. "Fifteen minutes of fame" was Andy Warhol's addition to Marshall McLuhan's "global village." Warhol predicted that in the global village, we would all be famous for fifteen minutes. I will return to this point, but many people get their fifteen minutes over and over again, with no one remembering you were the same person famous for fifteen minutes last year. Only the *really* famous stay that way. Media are fickle. Thank goodness.

2. There were also a lot of worried Canadian mothers (Voice of Women, et al). I met them decades later. They were the same mothers with the same Cold War memories.

CHAPTER 2

3. John Mitchell and Constance L. Stallings, eds, *Ecotactics: The Sierra Club Handbook for Environmental Activists* (New York: Simon & Schuster, 1970) pg. i.

4. Sierra Club of Canada often will take on new issues if there are volunteers with fresh energy to help. That way, a new issue gets the benefit of some experience while appropriating an established name.

5. Des Kennedy, *The Garden Club and the Kumquat Campaign* (Vancouver: Whitecap Books, 1996). Thanks to the author for use of this excerpt and for allowing me to edit.

6. Sierra Club, *Grassroots Organizing Training Manual,* (San Francisco: Sierra Club 1999). I always reflect on Chavez's success and his integrity. When he died in the 1990s, a virtual icon in the movement, his previous years' income had been six thousand dollars. I don't think anyone could say Bill Gates had been more successful.

CHAPTER 3

7. For a more complete account of the campaign to save South Moresby, see my book, *Paradise Won: The Struggle to Save South Moresby* (Toronto: McClelland and Stewart, 1990).

8. I shall return to the role that coincidence, psychic flashes, and, for lack of a better word, magic, can play in campaigns.

9. Warning: I don't let anyone else call me "Liz."

CHAPTER 5

10. David Shenk, *Data Smog: Surviving the Information Glut* (Toronto: HarperCollins, 1997).

CHAPTER 6

11. The ad was made possible with a grant from the Schad Foundation to cover shooting new footage and studio time. Anderson Advertising of Toronto donated the creative talent, and Sierra Club of Canada and the International Fund for Animal Welfare jointly developed the ad.

12. A particularly forceful example is the campaign to defeat the Multilateral Agreement on Investment (MAI), which was being negotiated through the Organization for Economic Cooperation and Development in 1998. The text was placed on the Web and groups all around the world shared information and developed a campaign that derailed the MAI.

13. I place coalition in quotes as that anti-Kyoto campaign, the Canadian Coalition for Environmentally Responsible Choices, was a bogus non-coalition. A few groups, the Council of CEOs and the Canadian Chamber of Commerce, masqueraded as a broader collection of industries.

CHAPTER 7

14. See appendix E for approved language for Parliamentary petitions. See also www.parl.gc.ca/info/guipete.html.

15. This is not to include the "police snatch"-style of arrest, where organizers are pulled from the street while peacefully minding their own business. The arrest of Jaghi Singh in Quebec City by plainclothes officers who forced him into a panel van

and hustled him into the night, leaving his terrified friends behind, is an inexcusable infringement on civil liberties.

16. For more of this discussion, see Using the Courts in chapter 9.

17. A "die-in" is a piece of theatre where demonstrators lie on the ground in mock "death" to symbolize the threats to human health from pollution or war.

18. A "critical mass" rally involves having so many bicycles in the city centre that no cars can drive down the streets. It is important to have permission and advance discussions with the police.

CHAPTER 8
19. See A Word on Brown Envelopes in chapter 4.

CHAPTER 9
20. Billie Shoecraft, *Sue the Bastards* (Phoenix: Franklin Press, 1971).

21. Trespass and public and private nuisance are causes of action in what is called tort law. Other torts include assault (civil, not criminal).

22. Charles Dickens, *Bleak House* (New York: Dutton, 1972), pg. 30.

23. There are a number of environmental law groups in Canada and the U.S. In the United States, the lead organization is called Earth Justice. Affiliated with Earth Justice in Canada is Sierra Legal Defence Fund (with no connection, historic or current, to Sierra Club of Canada. At this writing SLDF has announced it will change its name). Other Canadian groups include the Canadian Environmental Law Association (able to help clients in Ontario), Environmental Defence (helping support cases, but not providing counsel), West Coast Environmental Law, and the Environmental Law Centre of Alberta . (The last two do not provide legal counsel).

24. For more on environmental law in Canada, see David Estrin and John Swaigen's very helpful text, *Environment on Trial: A Guide to Ontario Environmental Law and Policy, 3rd ed.* (Toronto: Emond Montgomery, 1993); and Stephen Hazell's *Canada v. The Environment: Federal Environmental Assessment 1984–1998* (Toronto: Canadian Environmental Defence Fund, 1999), is very readable for the non-lawyer. Also see Rod Northey's more academic text, *The 1995 Annotated Canadian Enviromental Assessment Act* (Toronto: Carswell, 1994).

25. Particularly, U.S. politicians are just as likely as those in Canada to claim the matter is *sub jure* (before the courts) and cannot be discussed. Unless counsel is *pro bono* or working on a contingency arrangement, money issues are still a problem.

26. Jonathan Harr, *A Civil Action*, (New York: Random House, 1995). Nominated for a National Book Award, and awarded the National Book Critics Circle Award.

27. Betty Krawczyk, *Lock Me Up or Let Me Go: The Protests, Arrest and Trial of an Environmental Activist and Grandmother*, (Vancouver: Press Gang), 2002), pg. 13.

28. Ibid., pg. 190 The charge was reduced to four months on appeal.

29. Ibid, pg. 213.

30. Sierra Club in the U.S. and Sierra Club of Canada have, by their bylaws and constitutions, explicitly precluded themselves from any actions that are not legal. Sierra Club does not engage in civil disobedience.

31. Although clearly Prime Minister Trudeau had far more reason, in the throes of the FLQ crisis with the kidnapping and murder of cabinet ministers.

32. After it was all over, Dr. Donna Smyth wrote a wonderful memoir intermingled with a novel called *Subversive Elements* (Toronto: Toronto Women's Press, 1990).

33. In 1982, in the lawsuit against the use of Agent Orange in Nova Scotia's forests, we asked for a trial by jury, but we did not have an absolute right to one. The pulp company immediately made a motion for a trail by judge alone, which the same judge who ultimately ruled Agent Orange was safe, approved. He ruled that the issues would be far too complicated for the average person.

34. Our reasoning was that if the N.B. government had conducted a thorough advance review before permitting the incinerator, many of the issues being raised legitimately by Conservation Council would have been considered and the approval denied.

CHAPTER 10

35. Frederic March and Florence Eldridge were two of Hollywood's brightest stars in the 1930s and '40s. The first time we met I was at our literature table in 1968 for McCarthy. We had the usual buttons, pamphlets, and bumper stickers. Eldridge

picked up the bumper sticker and turned it over in her hands, examining it as if she'd never seen one before. She hadn't. I explained, "It's a bumper sticker." She called over, "Oh Freddie, come look! It is a *sticker* to put on the *bumper* of your car. How very clever!"

36. Ethiopia Airlift was a Halifax-based fundraising effort that shipped supplies to famine-stricken Ethiopia. Its creator was one of my classmates in law school, Peter Dalgleish, who went on to form Street Kids International. He was ably assisted by the then President of Kings College, John Godfrey, former Minister for Communities in the Martin cabinet.

CHAPTER 11

37. Presentation by Bobbi Speck, *Kyoto and Sprawl: Building Cities That Work*, conference at York University, July 25–27, 2003.

38. Norman Juster, *The Phantom Tollbooth* (New York: Epstein & Carroll, 1961).

39. Ibid., pg. 247.

40. Speck, p. 4

41. This is what Dalton Camp told me, based on my memory. Certainly, I learned in government that writing speeches was about more than addressing an audience for forty minutes. As Mulroney's press secretary, former newsman Bruce Phillips, once told me, "Policy making by speech writing is not dead."

42. The Earth Charter is an important and inspirational global effort. It is included in appendix C.

43. See the appendix F for the effective use of satire in the *Bush Briefing Book*.

44. Norman Cousins, *Anatomy of an Illness as Perceived by the Patient* (New York: W.W. Norton & Co., 2001), pg. 163.

INDEX

To learn more about
*How to Save the World
in your Spare Time*,
or to join us,
contact Sierra Club of Canada,
www.sierraclub.ca,
Suite 412, 1 Nicholas Street,
Ottawa, Ontario, K1N 7B7.

613-241-4611